WHY WE FAIL
LEARNING FROM EXPERIENCE DESIGN

Victor Lombardi

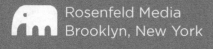
Rosenfeld Media
Brooklyn, New York

Why We Fail

Learning from Experience Design Failures

By Victor Lombardi

Rosenfeld Media, LLC

457 Third Street, #4R

Brooklyn, New York

11215 USA

On the Web: www.rosenfeldmedia.com

Please send errors to: errata@rosenfeldmedia.com

Publisher: Louis Rosenfeld

Developmental Editor: JoAnn Simony

Copyeditor: Ben Tedoff

Interior Layout: Danielle Foster

Cover Design: The Heads of State

Cover Illustration: John Gall

Indexer: Nancy Guenther

Proofreader: Kathy Brock

ISBN: 1-933820-17-9

ISBN-13: 978-1-933820-17-0

LCCN: 2013939950

Printed and bound in the United States of America

*For everyone brave enough to design into existence
something entirely new in the hope of improving our world*

HOW TO USE THIS BOOK

Who Should Read This Book?

Designers, product managers, project managers, marketers, and general managers will derive particular practical benefit from this book, as these are the roles I had in mind while writing. Yet I was careful to avoid unnecessary jargon so others with an interest in the technology industry can enjoy it as well.

What's in This Book?

Chapter 1, "Embrace Failure," starts with a story of one of my own professional failures. This first-person perspective will give you a sense of what that experience feels like as a product designer and how we can fail to learn from failure. I then argue that digital technology is becoming a vital part of everyday life and is too important to screw up. I show how we learn from failure, and how customer experience failure is new and different from engineering or design failure. Finally, I explain the criteria I used to select the case studies for this book.

Chapters 2 through 8 are the case studies. **Chapter 2**, "Get the Right Experience," includes the stories of BMW's iDrive telematics system and Google's Wave groupware service, illustrating how failure can originate early in the product development cycle, while still in the product concept stage.

Chapter 3, "Get the Experience Right," is about the OpenID authentication service and how rolling out an untested technology standard can lead to hundreds of years' worth of frustrating experience.

Chapter 4, "Platform Follows People," tells the story of Wesabe, a personal financial management service, and how a successful service with a cutting-edge strategy can be beaten by a competitor that focuses on a great customer experience.

Chapter 5, "Design for Reflection," is about the Microsoft Zune media player, a product every bit as good as its rival, but one that failed for social and cultural reasons.

Chapter 6, "Generate Critical Mass," compares Twitter to competitor Pownce and shows how a superior feature set doesn't always result in a superior experience.

Chapter 7, "Do the Right Thing," profiles the nostalgia site Classmates.com and the contact management service Plaxo. Both displayed ethically questionable business behavior that harmed their customers, yet their stories show that taking the high road isn't always as easy as making a decision to sacrifice some revenue.

Chapter 8, "Cannibalize Yourself," covers the Symbian mobile phone operating system and Apple's Final Cut Pro X video editing software, two products whose different rates of change pushed them in two different directions, both of which disappointed customers.

Chapter 9, "Why We Fail," synthesizes the underlying reasons for failed experience designs and points to quality-control methods from other industries to show a way forward.

Chapter 10, "Avoid Failure," reviews the recent history of applying quality-control ideas to design, software development, and business ventures, and then complements these with a method to avoid customer experience failure in our own work.

What Comes with This Book?

This book's companion website (rosenfeldmedia.com/books/why-we-fail/) contains a blog and other materials related to the book. The book's diagrams and other illustrations are available under a Creative Commons license (when possible) for you to download and include in your own presentations. You can find these on Flickr at www.flickr.com/photos/rosenfeldmedia/sets/.

FREQUENTLY ASKED QUESTIONS

What kinds of products are described in this book?

Of the ten products profiled in this book, four of them are websites (Classmates.com, Wave, Pownce, and Wesabe), two of them are services (Plaxo and OpenID), one is a software package (Final Cut Pro X), one is an operating system (Symbian), and two are hardware-based (iDrive and Zune). They were all generally created in the United States and Europe. All of them were designed for consumers rather than for businesses.

Why did you choose those products?

I began my research by surveying dozens of failed products—from small unheard-of start-ups to Boo.com, which spent more than $100 million; and from early consumer software such as WordStar to the most recent video games. I then focused on products that tried to innovate. There are certainly many examples of failed products that were attempts to copy others, or were simply incremental improvements over what came previously, but those cases aren't as interesting or instructive. I also excluded products that failed merely because the creators were incompetent or whose lessons are outdated or irrelevant. See Chapter 1 for a longer explanation.

How do you define "failure"?

The failures in this book are customer experience failures. The products somehow failed to offer their audiences a good experience. As a result, the product either failed in the marketplace (e.g., Symbian) or the company was forced to change the product to offer a better experience in order to survive in the marketplace (e.g., Plaxo). Chapter 1 has more examples of this definition.

Isn't a "customer experience failure" just another way to say it was a bad design?

This was often the case in the past when products were simpler and could be judged by their list of specifications, such as the speed of the processor or how many colors the screen could display. But today's digital products are so complex we engage with them differently. A product such as a smartphone may seem good based on how it looks and its list of specifications, and it might function perfectly fine, but we don't know if we like it until we try it. Our reasons for using these complex new products are multifaceted, and our experiences of them are emotional and subjective. They are *experiential products*, and they fail in *experiential* ways. In Chapter 1 I point to some videos that nicely illustrate the difference between *design* and *experience*.

Isn't there usually some other, underlying cause of the failure, such as hiring poorly trained designers?

Sometimes, but for this book I tried to find stories that revealed more interesting, less obvious lessons. For example, a product might work fine for one audience but fail when given to a different audience (e.g., OpenID). Or one aspect of the experience we think might be vital, such as a website that is always available, doesn't beat a competitor whose website is often down for maintenance (e.g., Pownce). Or two similar products might offer a similar experience to the consumer, but one might fail because of cultural and social reasons (e.g., Zune).

In any case, I also look behind the experiential reason for failure to find what caused that failure. See the "Why the Experience Failed" and "The Underlying Cause" sections in the Summaries that end Chapters 2 through 8.

Is experience design the main way products fail?

Products can fail for many reasons, from malfunctioning technology to ineffective marketing. This book focuses on customer experience failure because it's relatively new and not enough has been written about it to date.

Isn't learning from failure overrated?

There's an argument that says you should study your successes and then try to repeat those successes, making them a little better each time. That's fine if what you're doing is simple and is similar to something you've done in the past, such as designing a "Contact Us" form for a website. But what I see in the experience design field is change—a lot of change. Technology, products, customers' expectations, and culture are all changing quickly. To think we can only repeat what worked in the past is wishful thinking. I believe we need methods to help us understand customers' current experiences, quickly make design changes, and avoid failure on the product or project level. Chapter 1 has a longer explanation of why learning from failure is useful.

You recommend using a design process based on the scientific method, but how is that relevant to design?

First, because the scientific method is a universally understood, repeatable technique that underlies our civilization's massive progress since the 17th century. Design is about creating something that works for people, and we can use the scientific method for discovering if that something did indeed work.

Second, a reason the scientific method works well is because it seeks to remove psychological biases from our work by rationally and explicitly stating how our designs should work, how we will test them, and how we should evaluate the results of the tests. Chapter 9 discusses a host of psychological problems that lead to failure, and Chapter 10 outlines how to apply the scientific method to our work.

How can I use this book to avoid failure in my work?

There are at least three ways:

If you make a product similar to the ones in this book, you can directly apply the lessons learned. For example, if your product involves social networking, you and your colleagues should read Chapter 6 about Pownce. Then, as a group, study the key points in the Lessons and Summary sections at the end of the chapter. Compare them to your tactics and strategy to see if you might be making the same missteps.

Perhaps your products have started to be judged on their customers' experience rather than product performance (see explanation in Chapter 1). For example, television, musical instruments, home automation, and automobile telematics are product categories currently making this transition. If so, focus on Chapters 5 and 8 to learn from other product categories (mobile phones and media players) that made this transition. Then you may want to start applying the method described in Chapter 10 to develop and test your products with your customers' experience in mind.

If you've had failures in the past, you can conduct a postmortem to understand why the products failed and make changes to avoid failure in the future. Use the method in Chapter 10, particularly step 1 ("Understand the Customer Experience"), and refer to the Resources section at the back of the book for more specific guidance.

CONTENTS

FOREWORD

Embrace failure, avoid failure: these two, apparently contradictory statements are the opening and closing chapter titles of Victor Lombardi's enchanting, insightful book. Embrace, yet avoid—the apparent contradiction being resolved by recognizing that the trick is to learn from other people's failures, the better to be able to avoid them for yourself. The message of the book is summarized by its subtitle: *Learning from Experience Design Failures.*

Lots of people focus upon success, but failure is a far more effective teacher. I know this from my own experience: I've watched brilliant product releases such as Apple's QuickTake digital camera and Newton personal digital assistant. I was an advisor to the company that produced the first digital picture frame, licensed to Kodak and released as the Kodak Smart Picture Frame. You've probably never heard of these three products, which is understandable: they all failed in the marketplace. But I learned more about business from those failures than from all the things I have done that succeeded. Success can make people feel good. Failure can make people better. But failure is a learning experience only if it is treated as one, with a reflective review of all that went right and all that went wrong.

Reflective review—that's the power of this book. Fascinating case histories of product failures, coupled with careful analyses of the products themselves and, just as important, the marketing efforts and other components of their release and subsequent history. Lombardi doesn't just focus upon the failures and weaknesses. We learn of the strengths of each product—what was done right—as well as the weaknesses—what was done wrong. Thus, in a detailed analysis of Microsoft's Zune music player, its strengths and virtues are properly praised. The product was excellent. The failure lay in the auxiliary components of the product: how it was marketed, whether the advertising campaign was substantive and long-lasting enough to overcome the huge advantage already existing for the major competition. Lombardi makes clear that had Apple's iPod not existed, the Zune would have been declared a marvelous offering and probably would have gone on to a well-deserved, hefty success. Just having a great product is not sufficient.

Products do not exist in isolation: they need a supportive surrounding environment. And above all, they must deliver a compelling user experience, one that allows purchasers to get excited by the potential and to overlook the weaknesses that all new products have. Lots of books and articles have analyzed failure from the perspective of business, or the technical features and functions, or company management style. The real power of this book comes from the exemplary lessons on the importance of user experience, analyses from the point of view of the people who have to use the product. Experience is in the minds of the people, not in the product itself, which is one of the reasons that the product itself is not enough. Similarly, great design is not enough. Great design is indeed required to provide the framework for great experiences, but design alone cannot do the job. The psychological environment plays a critical role, which is why great marketing is essential. Experience is subjective and illusory. It is emotion. And in products, it is essential.

The power of *Why We Fail* is that it goes beyond the surface analysis of design, technology, or marketing. Instead, it treats all of these factors as an interconnected, related system. The analysis covers the entire product offering, providing a deep analysis of the many factors that go into success or failure.

The stories behind failures make for fascinating reading. But this book offers more. It provides important insights into both what can go right and what can go wrong in a product offering. To make great products, we need to understand what makes some fail and others succeed. To all the aspiring, young entrepreneurs who are reading this: take heed. Embrace failure to learn from failure. Learn from failure to avoid failure.

Don Norman
Co-founder, Nielsen Norman Group
Author of *The Design of Everyday Things* (Revised and Expanded)

CHAPTER 1

Embrace Failure

Ultimately, we are deluding ourselves if we think that the products that we design are the "things" that we sell, rather than the individual, social and cultural experience that they engender, and the value and impact that they have. Design that ignores this is not worthy of the name.

—Bill Buxton, computer scientist, designer, and a pioneer of the human–computer interaction field

Why I Failed

The year was 2000 and I was employed at a prestigious digital design agency working with a financial information company to create a new website that would revolutionize the research process for institutional investors, the people who manage investments for large companies and municipalities.

"Make it like a Bloomberg Terminal," is how the client summed it up. My team of designers and programmers winced at his suggestion because we considered the Bloomberg Terminal a powerful but ugly and difficult-to-learn interface design from the dark ages of text-based computers (Figure 1.1). We instead pushed him in the direction of beautiful charts and graphs, software agents that personalized information, and conventional Web navigation that would be familiar to his clients.

FIGURE 1.1
A Bloomberg Terminal.

Our client hadn't actually done any research with his customers to understand if they would like his ideas. And neither had we. He was leaning on his expertise in managing similar products and we were leaning on our experience having designed similar products, but neither of us had validated these particular ideas with these particular customers. At the time, the methods we had for validating our ideas were not compellingly useful, and perhaps my team and the client implicitly understood this. We made minimal effort to conduct research with the client's customers, and he denied us access to them.

With each stage of the project the design and technology accumulated more flaws. When the client decided the team was wrong for the job, another team at my agency replaced us. After more missteps the client's upper management replaced their team. Eventually the whole project was canceled; the client's company decided to use off-the-shelf software instead, which was never a success with its customers. In the end the project was a failure, all too common in the early days of the Web.

Ouch. I was a young designer and had never experienced a big failure at work. I felt terrible. No one at our agency wanted to focus on the failures and take time to discuss them, so the team never understood why we failed. Without a good explanation and without something tangible I could do to improve, I sometimes felt depressed and I lost confidence in my skills. Sometimes I became defensive and blamed the "dumb client."

But I saw that things around me were even worse: clients were firing agencies after as little as a month or clients were suing agencies. Some of the mistakes agencies were making were to be expected. The Internet represented a new world of design and technology that changed on a daily basis. Everyone was learning and experimenting; there were no experts.

Since the time of that first early failure, I've contributed to or directly managed over 40 Internet and software projects, some as a designer and some as a product manager. There have been other failures, and even when I understand why I failed it still takes an emotional toll. In spite of my own failures, you'll see as you read this book that I'm often a harsh critic of my peers' work. I don't criticize because I think leading a design project from start to finish is easy. It's not. It's hard work. I criticize the outcomes I see *because* it's hard work and because failure is still too common. I want all of us to get it right more often, with less of the emotional toll of failure. I hope by reading this book and applying the lessons learned, avoiding failure will be easier for you and those you work with.

I failed mostly because I didn't have the right methods to discover which of our ideas would give customers an experience they wanted. Since then, those methods have improved significantly.

Why This Stuff Is Really Important

I see the trend of our work going beyond the ubiquitous convenience it is today and becoming a vital part of the infrastructure supporting life in the 21st century. Currently most of our work complements or enhances life; people don't rely on it as essential yet. An updated status on Facebook, an e-mail to a friend, accessing information on websites . . . if all this were turned off tomorrow people would feel inconvenienced, but they could find work-arounds for all of it.

But that's changing rapidly. I now make appointments with my doctor online, and the doctor transmits my prescription for medicine directly to my pharmacist online (Figure 1.2). I pay the doctor, the pharmacist, and the health insurance online. As people become accustomed to this way of working—and as service providers become accustomed to the efficiency, accuracy, and cost savings—the old ways will gradually be discontinued. Increasingly, we will rely on digital products and services for everyday matters of life and death.

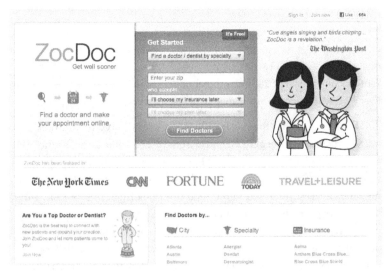

FIGURE 1.2
With ZocDoc, patients can find a doctor, see the doctor's schedule, and make an appointment.

We are each the product of our experience. The things we do, the places we go, the people we meet, and *the things we use* all influence who we are. Over time, as we interact with more and more technology to live our lives, we will spend more of our time looking at screens, and the quality of the design of this technology will have ever greater influence on the quality of our lives.

Why We Learn from Failure

Instead of studying failures, can't we just study successes and then repeat whatever led to those successes? Yes, this is a good tactic in very simple situations, such as learning how to tie your shoes. There's not much to be gained by looking at how many ways it's possible to tie your shoes incorrectly. If you fail, nothing terrible happens.

Any industry that's important, complex, and dynamic takes the time to examine failures. Aviation, medicine, and manufacturing are three fields that have taught us an enormous number of lessons by studying failures.

Here's a good example. During World War II a mathematician in the United States named Abraham Wald worked on the problem of deciding where to add additional armor to B-29 bomber planes to keep them from getting shot down. Looking at planes that had successfully returned from flying missions, he determined statistically where the bullets had hit the planes and plotted the locations, as represented schematically in Figure 1.3.

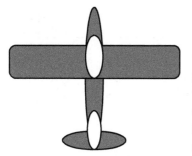

FIGURE 1.3
The dark regions indicate where enemy bullets hit the B-29 bombers in World War II that successfully returned home.

The initial reaction to this data might be, "We need to add additional armor to the dark areas because that's where the bullets are hitting the planes." Wald's insight was that the planes with bullet holes in the dark areas returned successfully, so perhaps the planes that did not return were shot down because they had bullet holes in the light areas. His recommendation was to *add armor to the light areas instead.*

As a statistician, Wald would naturally want to make a decision based on a random sample of all planes, but he didn't have access to the planes that were shot down. He understood the limitation of his sample and adjusted for it. He successfully dodged *survivorship bias*, the mistake of learning only from the survivors of some process.

Survivorship bias happens all the time. Witness the marketing hype in our industry that, devoid of research, hails every new method and technology as the fix for people's business or personal needs. It seems easier to research and analyze companies and products that currently exist instead of searching for information on companies and products that have perished. Doing so can lead us to believe that the survivors have some special quality that helps them survive, when it's possible they were just lucky (Figure 1.4).

FIGURE 1.4
Survivorship bias
as employed by the
satirical news website
The Onion.

The lesson here is very simple: to increase your chances of success and lower your chances of failure, you need to carefully examine cases of both success and failure.

Why Experience Failure Is Different

So we know why studying failure is important, but do we really need another book on failed products? Yes we do, because previous books were about *design* rather than *experience*.

To help illustrate the difference, I'll group the many design-related failures into three broad categories:

1. **Engineering failure:** The product physically fails to function as designed.

2. **Design failure:** The product physically works, but is so badly designed people can't use it.

3. **Experience failure:** The product physically works and people can use it, but using it is an undesirable experience.

For engineering failure, we have great studies of how and why things fail in physical ways, most notably Henry Petroski's studies of buildings, bridges, and pyramids, as in his book *Success through Failure: The Paradox of Design*. But studying a bridge that failed is worlds apart from studying a failed website. When people use bridges, they don't directly interact with them the same way they interact with digital products. For example, a sleeping passenger in a car can pass over a bridge without even knowing it, whereas people actively and directly interact with digital products (Figure 1.5). I've never heard of a bridge that was torn down and replaced because people didn't like it much. But in this age of plentiful digital products, people have enough options to be selective about what they use.

FIGURE 1.5
On August 1, 2007, the Interstate 35W bridge in Minneapolis collapsed. The 1961 design could not handle the load that had increased over time. The lessons learned from this failure are valuable but only vaguely applicable to digital products.

In the second case, design failure, the product physically works but its design makes it too hard to use. We used to call this "human error" but the more common term in the fields of ergonomics and human factors is now "design-induced error," which moves the blame from the people using the product to the people who designed it. Whenever you're using any kind of computer and feel confused about how to use it correctly, you're experiencing design-induced error. Many of us are old enough to remember trying in vain to set the digital clock on our VCRs. This is a classic example of a design-induced problem (Figure 1.6).

FIGURE 1.6
Trying in vain to set the digital clock on VCRs was a classic design-induced problem of the 1980s and 1990s.

Having a product break and feeling confused by a design are definitely things people still experience, but interactive digital products are more sophisticated now. They do more than just perform simple functions like recording a TV show at a particular time. They connect us socially, they allow us to shop and conduct business from home, and they smooth a million transactions from navigating a car to finding a book at the library. Mere usability is a low bar for these products to clear; they now aim much higher, engaging our higher-level functions and sometimes even engaging us emotionally.

While the concept of design-induced error is a useful subset of failure I'll look at in this book, experience failure comprises much more.

In this book I will talk about *design*—the appearance and behavior of a product—separately from the *experience*—people's thoughts, feelings, and actions while using the product. I illustrate this distinction explicitly in Chapter 8 with the case of Nokia's Symbian S60 mobile phone operating system. The Symbian-based phones had a long list of features and high-performance specifications that sounded great on paper, but the iPhone and Android phones offered a more pleasing experience, despite having far fewer features. With the first iPhone you couldn't even spell-check your e-mail or customize your ringtone, and yet it sold very well. Consumer electronics have now reached a performance threshold where more features and performance offer diminishing returns unless the design helps people have a good experience.

One observer has called this "the death of the spec,"[1] meaning the list of specifications is no longer as important as the experience. This phrase was coined as a result of "Antennagate," the controversy over the signal reception of Apple's iPhone 4 in July 2010. *Consumer Reports* magazine evaluated the phone and found that holding it a certain way would significantly reduce the signal strength, a potentially fatal flaw for a mobile phone.[2] The magazine, usually content to simply publish ratings and move on, went further and issued several news updates, even calling on Apple to fix the problem (Figure 1.7).

FIGURE 1.7

Of the iPhone 4 from Apple, *Consumer Reports* said, "Despite all its strengths, we can't recommend this phone due to the signal-reception problem we confirmed during testing." Despite this review, Apple sold a record number of iPhones. Watch the video at http://rfld.me/WQDju5.

You might assume with all the publicity about a fundamental flaw in the iPhone 4 that sales would plummet. For the fiscal quarter ending September 25, 2010, Apple sold 14.1 million iPhones, which was 91 percent more iPhones than the same quarter from the previous year.[3] Apparently people who wanted the iPhone 4 decided to buy it against the advice of independent product experts. This massive contrast between the publicity of the defect and the record sales numbers served to highlight the death of the spec of interactive digital products.

Marco Arment, a software developer and technology writer, offered this explanation for the situation:

> For [*Consumer Reports*'] ratings to be useful to my purchase, their priorities and criteria need to approximately match mine. This is easy for most of the products they review: . . . An air conditioner that uses less energy for the same cooling is better than a less efficient model. You can assign numbers and scores to factors like these.
>
> Smartphones have too many subjective criteria, and even the measurable stats don't always yield a definite answer on what's better. If you want a huge screen, you'll get a huge phone, so is a larger screen size a good thing or not? Fast 4G network access kills battery life, so is 4G a good feature for you? . . . These all depend on your priorities.
>
> A product as complex and multifaceted as a modern smartphone is beyond *Consumer Reports*' ability to rate in a way that's useful to most buyers.[4]

Subjective is the word that stands out for me here. While the qualities of a design can be objectively described on a list of specifications, the qualities of people's experience—their thoughts and feelings about a complex, multifaceted product—are subjective.

And that's one thing about designing digital products these days that is different and, I think, trickier. We just don't know if they work or not until we evaluate the subjective experience of the people using them. Sure, we can check if the products function correctly and ask independent experts to review them. But the products we're now making are *experiential products*, and only the people experiencing them know if they are ultimately successful or not (Figure 1.8).

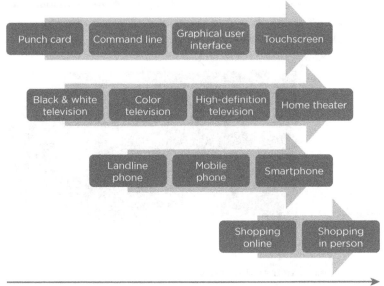

More Experiential

FIGURE 1.8

Adding screens, richer graphics, audio, and direct manipulation (e.g., touchscreens) makes technology more experiential. Some tasks such as shopping can be more efficient online but less experiential than the offline equivalent.

Why Design ≠ Experience

To fully understand the failures cited in this book, I describe both the product design and the outcome of that design—the experience. Ultimately it is in the experience that these products fail, but by presenting both the design and the experience I hope to illuminate the difference and help you completely appreciate the lessons learned.

Even though I've been working in the "experience design" industry for years, this design/experience dichotomy hasn't been easy for me to arrive at. Because we so often use the word "experience" to describe the design, it takes some conceptual backflips to think about a person's experience apart from the product.

To help you see the difference between design and experience here are two automotive examples. I like taking examples from the automotive world because most people are familiar with cars. Figure 1.9 is a still from a video describing the *design* of a new concept car. The reporter discusses the styling, the price, and the business issues at the automaker, but not the *experience* of what it's like to drive the vehicle. This is only a concept vehicle and the reporter didn't have access to a working prototype.

FIGURE 1.9
In this video about a Lamborghini concept vehicle, the reporter discusses the design but not the experience. Watch the video at http://rfld.me/WTeCwY.

Contrast that with the video of an off-road rally car driver taking a passenger for a short ride (Figure 1.10). We don't know where they are, who they are, or how fast they're going. We don't know anything about the design of the car other than the little we can see in the blurry video. But we know the woman in the passenger seat is ecstatic, smiling throughout the entire four-minute ride, laughing and uttering curses as she's bumped and tossed around. That's *experience*.

FIGURE 1.10
You can appreciate her experience of riding in a rally car without knowing anything about the design of the car. Watch the video at http://rfld.me/XqAteu.

Here's a parallel example relevant to software. Figure 1.11 is a still from a video I made highlighting an interesting design aspect of Microsoft Office 2007. It's all about design and not at all about experience.

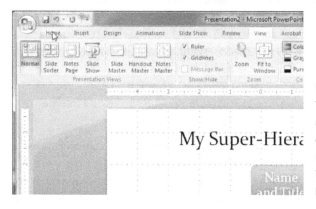

FIGURE 1.11
The design (but not the experience) of the ribbon in Microsoft Office. Watch the video at http://rfld.me/YWgU4C.

Next is a video compilation of disabled people interacting with Drupal websites (Figure 1.12). We can't tell much about the design of the websites from the video, but we get to see people's reactions as they use the sites and later reflect on the experience.

FIGURE 1.12
People's experiences with Drupal websites. Watch it at http://rfld.me/11siEnB.

This focus on experience isn't new, but only recently has it started to become more widespread as a concept. The seminal work on experience as an economic force is *The Experience Economy* by Joseph Pine II and James H. Gilmore, first published in 1999. They observed that "companies stage an experience whenever they engage customers, connecting with them in a personal, memorable way."[5] They argue that experiences are an economic force just like commodities, goods, and services, which can be intentionally produced, consumed, and measured.

One reason for isolating experiences is that they are profitable. For example, Pine and Gilmore show how the profit margin for coffee increases along a value chain. The raw beans to make a cup of coffee (a commodity) cost 1 or 2 cents, but when a manufacturer roasts, grinds, and packages the coffee for sale (a good) the price to a consumer increases to as much as 25 cents. A brewed cup of coffee at a quick service restaurant (a service) can increase the value to between 50 cents and a dollar. Starbucks deliberately aims for a highly engaging experience—by preparing special beverages and serving them in an environment enhanced with interior design, music, and Internet access—and receives $2 to $5 for a cup of coffee.[6]

Compared with commodities, goods, and services, the consumer price index shows that people are paying increasingly more for experiences.[7] Experiences also show a faster rate of growth when contributing to both employment and gross domestic product (GDP).[8]

As competition in various industries increases, companies sometimes try to move up this value chain, turning their commodities, goods, and services into experiences and seeking higher profit margins. For example,

> Glimcher Realty Trust, which owns and manages shopping malls, is experimenting with making them Internet-proof. The company concedes that if shoppers can buy something online, they will. So it is trying to fill one of its malls, in Scottsdale, Ariz., with businesses that do more than sell stuff.
>
> There are still clothing-only retailers at the mall, Scottsdale Quarter, but more than half of the stores offer dining or some other experience that cannot be easily replicated on the Web. That has Glimcher executives taking some unconventional approaches to finding suitable tenants—like testing out laser salons, getting hairstyling lessons, and watching movies in a theater that serves food.
>
> "It's retail Darwinism," Mr. Glimcher said.[9]

Nathan Shedroff's book *Experience Design* is the seminal introduction to the design of digital, experiential products. First published in 2001, the touchstone work ranges broadly from interaction design to designing for the senses. Here's how Shedroff describes the state of the field:

The design of experiences isn't any newer than the recognition of experiences. As an approach, though, Experience Design is still in its infancy. Simultaneously having no history (since it has, still, only recently been defined), and the longest history (since it is the culmination of many, ancient disciplines), Experience Design has become newly recognized and named. However, it is really the combination of many previous disciplines; but never before have these disciplines been so interrelated, nor have the possibilities for integrating them into whole solutions been so great.[10]

Both *The Experience Economy* and *Experience Design* argue that a product or service is designed, sold, and used differently than an experience.

One reason we can turn our attention to our audience's experience is that we're less challenged to design technology to satisfy basic functions. Before, we had to work hard to design interfaces that could compensate for performance shortcomings, whereas now we sometimes have more computing speed, communications bandwidth, and storage than we generally require. The *experiential threshold* is crossed when technology reaches a point of sophistication where product design can engage people's emotions. A recent example is the portable music player. In the 1980s portable cassette players like the Walkman let people take their music with them, but the devices themselves didn't engage their emotions (Figure 1.13). In the 2000s digital music players transformed that experience by storing people's entire music collection in their pockets and adding interactive screens, especially touchscreens (Figure 1.14). Suddenly the range of interactions increased dramatically. Sliding a finger on a screen allows an infinite number of input possibilities, and the devices can use graphics and sound to communicate back to the user, becoming so much more than just music players.[11]

FIGURE 1.13
A Sony Walkman circa 1998.

FIGURE 1.14
An Apple iPod Touch
circa 2012.

This concept of the experiential threshold is gradually permeating the technology media. For example when Microsoft released its Windows Surface tablets in June 2012, Darren Murph at *Engadget* wrote,

> Microsoft's playing coy when it comes to both CPU speed and available memory. Not unlike Apple and its iPad, actually. We're guessing that the company will try to push the user experience instead of focusing on pure specifications, and it's frankly about time the industry started moving in that direction. Pure hardware attributes only get you so far, and judging by the amount of integration time that went into this project, Microsoft would be doing itself a huge disservice to launch anything even close to not smooth-as-butter.[12]

Because people relate to experiential products differently, each product fails differently. It might fail because we feel overwhelmed (Google Wave) or underwhelmed (Microsoft Zune). We might feel cheated (Classmates.com) or annoyed (Plaxo). We might feel frustrated (OpenID) or maddened (BMW iDrive). We might become enlightened to a need we didn't know we had, and then realize that another, different product would actually satisfy this need better (Pownce, Wesabe).

Why You Should Keep Reading This Book

What all the stories in this book have in common is that the products somehow failed to offer their audience a good experience. As a result the product either failed in the marketplace (e.g., Symbian) or the company was forced to change the product to offer a better experience in order to survive in the marketplace (e.g., Plaxo). The stories are sometimes sad, sometimes surprising, and sometimes enraging. But each one taught me something valuable about how to do my work, and I hope they will do the same for you.

I limited the case studies in this book to digital products, in particular software and consumer electronics. All the products examined here tried to innovate in one way or another before failing. There are certainly examples of failed products that attempted to copy others or simply to make incremental improvements over what came previously, but those cases aren't as interesting or instructive. I also excluded products that failed merely because the creators were incompetent or the lessons are outdated or irrelevant.

My key message in this book is this: experience design is an incredibly young field and we have much to learn about how people experience our products. However, there has been work over the past decades to address the challenges faced in this book, and the lessons others have learned can help us avoid failure.

CHAPTER 2

Get the Right Experience

According to Bill Buxton, the pioneer computer scientist and designer, there's a difference between "getting the design right and getting the right design."[1] To get a design right, we can test it with customers and integrate their feedback by altering the design. But how do we know that what we started with is what customers want at all? I think of it this way: if we only test bottle openers, we may never realize customers prefer screw-top bottles. That's what Buxton means by getting *the right design.*

In a study, Buxton and his colleagues found that testing multiple alternative designs not only helped to select the superior design but also resulted in people voicing "more and stronger criticisms."[2] This feedback is especially important when attempting to successfully reinvent a product category with an entirely new design.

In our context of experiential products, the parallel is true: *Get the experience right, and get the right experience.* Here are two stories of products with radical new designs that launched, encountered severe customer experience problems, and then had to struggle to get the design right, because both had started with the wrong design.

BMW iDrive

This Is Your Grandfather's Dashboard

In 1901 the first mass-produced gasoline automobile was named for one of its most important features: the Oldsmobile Curved Dash (Figure 2.1).[3] Dashboards in cars were a design feature borrowed from horse and buggies, where they kept the dirt kicked up by the horse from hitting passengers and their clothing. The fundamental purpose of the first dashboards was to protect the driver.

As cars became more sophisticated with devices like ignition switches and gauges to measure electrical current and speed, the logical location for these devices was bolted to the dashboard where the driver could easily see and reach them. By the bronze age of automobiles, starting in 1905, the dashboard was firmly established in cars from the American Ford Model T in 1908 to the French Bugatti in 1910. Within decades the arrangement of gauges and controls we're familiar with today became convention, and from the 1940s, design of the dashboard was more a matter of style than utility. In the 1970s, automakers experimented with LED-powered digital gauges, mostly to ill effect, and subsequently retreated from these (Figure 2.2). By the 1980s, dashboards were mostly an analog affair sprinkled with occasional digital readouts.

FIGURE 2.1
A 1902 Oldsmobile
Model R Curved Dash
kept mud off your duds.

FIGURE 2.2
All-digital dashboards, such as this cathode-ray-powered example in an Aston Martin Lagonda, were abandoned because of poor readability and difficult maintenance.

The Rise of Telematics

As the 21st century approached, luxury automakers faced a technical design challenge: an ever increasing array of new in-car devices—phone, GPS navigation, digital radio, satellite radio, CD changers, Internet access, television, emergency notification, side and rearview cameras, and driving system settings—were turning dashboards into an unfathomable mess. Worse, new technologies were emerging at a faster pace than ever before and it was harder to design an automobile interior that would accommodate unpredictable future technologies. A new term, *vehicle telematics*, was coined to encompass this array of technology.

Deep inside the car was a similar advance in technology. Computers called electronic control units were increasingly used to control the engine, the transmission, the suspension, and many other vehicle systems.

Add to this challenge the need to follow government regulations that dictate vehicle telematics guidelines for in-car information and communication systems. There are several different major sets of guidelines from European, Japanese, and American government agencies, as well as from the international Society of Automotive Engineers.

If you sum this design challenge—telematics, future proofing, electronic control units, and regulation—you can understand how an automaker would want to control this chaos by unifying the computers into one system. And once you've done that, it's a short mental leap to imagine a unified interface for the customer to operate this computer system. This point of view represented the bold thought that a new age of telematics had arrived and it was time to make a clean break from the past.

The Ultimate Driving Minimalism

In 2002 BMW's 7 series was their top-of-the-line offering, a large sedan that sold for about $70,000. It was a tour de force of automotive design and technology. The long list of features even included a brake-drying feature that periodically wiped the brakes dry when the windshield wipers were in use. And when *Automobile* magazine compared the 7 series to counterparts from Mercedes-Benz, Jaguar, and Audi, the reviewers said the BMW had the edge in pure over-the-road driving behavior.

But when the reviewers focused on iDrive, a telematics system that was introduced in this model, they found this one aspect of the car not only detracted from the driving experience but went so far as to jeopardize the fundamental brand proposition:

> The BMW 745Li should be the numero uno in this test, but its excellent performance at the test track and its even more impressive performance on challenging country roads are badly offset by iDrive. The iDrive system represents a layer

of complexity that actually detracts from what ought to be a breathtaking driving experience. BMW bills itself as "the ultimate driving machine," and our test car would have been all that and more without the iDrive.

. . . The BMW demonstrated that ultra-high tech improperly managed is actually a detriment to a great road car with great performance.[4]

BMW wasn't the first company to attempt such a system. Mercedes-Benz had introduced their COMAND system two years earlier, striving to integrate communications (mobile phone and emergency roadside assistance), audio, and GPS navigation into one interface (Figure 2.3). The array of buttons and voice recognition features were so difficult to learn and use that the popular British automobile television program *Top Gear* openly mocked its poor performance.[5]

FIGURE 2.3
The 2000 Mercedes COMAND system was an early attempt to integrate communications, audio, and navigation systems.

Never a company to shy away from bold designs, BMW met the telematics challenge with a radical solution: remove almost all buttons, knobs, and switches that aren't actually needed to drive the car and replace them with a single dial, called the controller. The controller was located on the console between the two front seats and acted like a pointing device to select choices on an LCD screen on the dashboard (Figure 2.4). The on-screen choices were in hierarchical menus (Figure 2.5). To watch BMW's video introduction to iDrive, go to http://rfld.me/XXqv4e.

FIGURE 2.4
The iDrive controller.

FIGURE 2.5
The iDrive display.

The 7 series also offered voice recognition so that a driver could set the GPS by simply saying an address out loud. But the driver was required to learn to speak specific commands, and even then the system frequently had such difficulty interpreting the words, it was lampooned on the National Public Radio show *All Things Considered* in the United States.[6]

The iDrive concept was a wonderful techno-utopian dream—the driver could lean back and with a mere flick of the wrist access hundreds of settings via the computer screen set in an elegant dashboard. Aesthetically and logically the design made perfect sense. BMW could integrate several different subsystems into one system, and unknown future functions could be added via software, all controlled through the one central controller and screen. It also looked beautiful, returning the dashboard to an aesthetic simplicity reminiscent of cars from an earlier era. But what looked good as a design on paper was different as an experience in the driver's seat.

The iDrive Customer Experience

Let's compare part of a driver's typical experience using a pre-2002 conventional dashboard with that of using the iDrive. On first settling into a car with a conventional dashboard, your initial impression wouldn't amount to much, as you've seen the familiar layout many times before. On sitting in a BMW with iDrive, you would immediately notice the elegant minimalist controls, the modern display screen, and the invitingly designed rotary dial underneath your right hand. In a conventional car, you start the engine and press a preset button on the radio to choose a radio station. With iDrive, you would start the engine and then wait about 30 seconds while the computer boots up the Windows CE operating system. Then you'd read the initial screen on the display asking you to "use this system only when traffic conditions permit" and push the controller down to accept this warning. Then you'd tilt the controller to navigate to the Entertainment menu, rotate the controller to highlight a radio band (like FM) and press the controller down to select it, then rotate the controller to highlight the Presets menu and press down to select it, and then rotate to select your radio station preset and press down to select it. In a conventional car, selecting a preset radio station requires one action; with iDrive it required seven.

In a conventional car, the electronics can easily function reliably for the life of the car. iDrive, because it was a computer running software, would crash once in a while, requiring a reboot that was performed by restarting the car. And as with a desktop computer, the manufacturer occasionally released software updates and recommended that you install them, in this case requiring a visit to the dealer.

That was your experience if you had already taken some time to become accustomed to iDrive. If not, you would need time to learn the menu structure and develop a muscle memory of when to rotate, when to tilt, and when to press down. Don't forget, you may have been doing this while driving your 4,486-pound car down a rain-slicked highway at 65 mph while carrying on a conversation with a passenger and drinking coffee. Also consider that the "you" in demographic terms was an older, wealthy driver who was statistically less familiar with computers.

In 2002 iDrive simply required much more effort than drivers were accustomed to, or had come to expect. I'm not surprised by the reaction iDrive got after it launched. Customers ranted for years about their experience. For example:

> This stoopid knob controls everything - stereo, temperature, nav, etc. you can push it, pull it, turn it . . . so so so dumb and non intuitive. my dad yelled at me when i changed the radio station because he knew there was no way he'd be able to change it back on his own.
>
> —"dpstyles," Flickr[7]

> I hate the iDrive in my BMW with a passion. It goes against all common sense. Specifically, a new invention should work the way people think or it becomes a distraction. While you're driving, that's deadly. iDrive is BMW's stupid control-knob which you turn, press, or push/pull in one of four directions to make things happen. My previous vehicle (Acura MDX) had a touch screen so everything is in front of your face. [The control-knob shouldn't be on] the PASSENGER side of the console. What idiot came up with that?
>
> —Eric Seiden, The Quagmire[8]

Two of the most prominent interface design experts in the world also took time to critique the iDrive:

> Here are just few examples of the BMW 745i's clueless interaction design: Response times . . . Clumsy task flows . . . Misleading mapping . . . Obscure abbreviations . . . Lack of situational awareness . . .
>
> —Jakob Nielsen[9]

It is indeed true that the number of displays and controls on the modern automobile dashboard have grown over the years. But the solution is better design, not hiding them away in a complex menu structure. . . . I am appalled.

—Don Norman[10]

Although a few in the media praised the logic of the design, the vast majority bashed it. For example:

A total disaster.

—Edward Loh, executive editor of *Motor Trend*[11]

I am officially denouncing iDrive as a failure from both a technical and functional standpoint.

—Karl Brauer, Edmunds.com[12]

Run by a HAL 9000.

—Aaron Robinson, *Car and Driver*[13]

The criticism was about more than annoying lack of usability. Critics were concerned for drivers' safety:

After a bit of this, you may wonder what's the fuss over handheld cellphones . . . with [iDrive's] simple functions buried in menus and obscured by cryptic labels like "Auto P" and "PDC PIC." iDrive is capable of managing more than 700 functions, but I can't imagine more than a few dozen things I'd want a car to do. Even if a modern automobile is essentially a mobile computer, its operator's first concern is to keep it from crashing.

—James G. Cobb, *New York Times*[14]

Most annoying was the needlessly complex iDrive control system, which we found distracting and judged potentially dangerous to use when driving.

—*Consumer Reports*[15]

> The actual car—the bit that all this trickery is designed to
> control—is a superb work of automotive engineering. By
> adding an uber gizmo, The Boys From Bavaria have revealed a
> bizarre lack of confidence in and focus on their core values. The
> company that builds "The Ultimate Driving Machine" is the one
> company that should know an over-complicated and dangerous
> distraction when it sees one. The iDrive is not, as BMW claims,
> "A New Way to Drive." It is, in fact, a new way to die.
>
> —Robert Farago, The Truth About Cars[16]

The dashboard, whose original purpose was protection, was now threatening to harm its passengers.

What BMW Got Right

For all its faults, there were certainly some positive aspects of the iDrive design.

Controller Placement

BMW designers consciously located controls so the driver could easily reach them without having to lean out of the seat, placing all nondriving controls on the lower middle of the dashboard and on the console between the seats. By locating the controller dial between the seats, it fell directly under the right hand in a completely natural arm position, a position later copied by Mercedes and Audi.

Industrial Design and Haptic Feedback

The controller itself had indentations around the outer rim to make it easy to grip. And when turned, the controller provided haptic feedback, vibrating or providing subtle resistance to reinforce the on-screen feedback. When rotating the controller through a menu, a slight "bump" would be felt as the cursor passed over each item. The haptic feedback could simulate the feel of different real-world dials, from an audio bass dial when adjusting the stereo to a camera's zoom lens when zooming in and out on maps. Experienced drivers could perform some functions relying mostly on haptic feedback, reducing the need to take their eyes off the road and look at the screen.

Dedicated Controls

Although iDrive absorbed almost all nondriving controls, there were three functions deemed vital—adjusting the temperature, the fan speed, and audio volume—that had dedicated controls on the dashboard.

Extensible Software

The system did prove able to incorporate more features in later versions, a key benefit of embodying functions in software instead of hardware controls.

Pleasurable Design

Some devices are attractive because they look good or feel good, or because having them makes us feel empowered, and this was the case with iDrive. The controller felt great in the hand. Using a screen to adjust settings, and even the *idea* of iDrive, felt like living in the future. Drivers could even check the engine oil level while sitting comfortably inside the car. It might require 10 minutes to find the menu while turning and pressing the controller dozens of times, but to anyone who has ever had to lean over an engine to check the oil level using a greasy dipstick, the iDrive method was a joy. And even if you never used iDrive to check the oil level, it was fun to brag to your neighbor that you could. When not causing frustration due to usability problems, iDrive had the power to delight.

What BMW Got Wrong

Unfortunately, the list of iDrive's vices is longer and quite damning.

Unfamiliar Controls

People can quickly intuit how something works, such as a doorknob they've never seen before, because they've seen and used other doorknobs and have built up a familiarity with how doorknobs work, an intuition, over the course of years.[17] The same is true for conventional dashboard controls, which have evolved slowly over the past 100 years. iDrive could have retained more of the familiar dashboard controls while gradually introducing software-based functions, as other automakers did, but instead BMW replaced almost everything with an unfamiliar system. BMW called iDrive intuitive, but actually it was the opposite of intuitive.

Cognitive Overload

When drivers use a familiar automotive control, such as the brake pedal, they don't have to think about it or even see it; they use muscle memory to remember exactly how to press the pedal. Drivers build up muscle memory of physical dashboard controls as well, but this was much harder to do with iDrive. Though the haptic feedback helped slightly, iDrive generally required looking at the screen, taking attention away from driving, a significant safety concern. As design expert Don Norman warned, "The challenge presented by automobile driving is that attentional demands are so uneven: mostly very light and then, oftentimes with little warning, extremely heavy, requiring responses measured in fractions of a second. Because it is not easy to predict when the attention will be required, the only safe way to drive is always to be undistracted, with complete attention to the task."[18]

No Progressive Disclosure

iDrive's on-screen settings were sorted into categories such as Entertainment, Climate, Communication, and Car Data, which probably seemed logical when reviewed on paper. The problem was that when all of the settings were neatly categorized by topic, frequent tasks like selecting a preset radio station weren't any easier to access than infrequent tasks like changing the language of the display. iDrive was criticized for cramming more than 700 settings into the system, but this was a problem only because the menu structure didn't make frequent settings faster to access. If the iDrive menus located less common features an additional step away, it would have reduced distraction and simplified the display, an interface design technique known as *progressive disclosure*.

Invisible Behavior

Because navigating the menu structure required so many extra steps to perform common functions, the software designers created shortcuts based on assumptions about what they thought drivers would want. Here's an example from the manual about selecting a radio station: "Each time you confirm "AM" the system alternately switches between the AM waveband and the "Autostore" mode. Each time you confirm "FM" the system alternately switches between "Memorized Station" and the "Autostore" mode."[19]

If you think that's confusing to read, it was just as confusing to use, and could easily send drivers into Autostore mode when they had no intention of being there. Autostore automatically stored into presets the strongest radio stations in the area, replacing any stations already manually saved in presets.

Brevity Trumped Clarity

Usability expert Jakob Nielsen summed it up: "Although the designers have a fairly big screen at their disposal, they've littered the UI with commands like 'DSC/DTC,' 'BC,' 'Avoid sect.,' 'WB,' and 'Recirc. air MFL.' What they mean is anybody's guess. Better to spell out the commands when you have the space (for example, 'Weather' instead of 'WB')."[20]

Too Slow

Sometimes after pressing the iDrive controller, there would be a delay for a few seconds before the next screen was displayed. We know from decades of usability research that people feel the system is reacting instantaneously if feedback happens within one-tenth of a second, and for the flow of thought to stay uninterrupted requires feedback within one second.[21] Delays that hurt usability are unfortunate when sitting in your driveway, but they are simply dangerous in a moving car. When it came to GPS navigation, sometimes the display didn't keep up with turns the car was making.

Conversely, drivers who became adept at operating the controller reported that the screen couldn't keep up and when it finally reacted would misinterpret the input from the controller, resulting in displaying the wrong screen or entering a wrong value.

Odd Redundancy

The 7 series had two CD players in the dashboard: a six-CD changer operated by iDrive and a single disc player operated manually. If iDrive was so great, why incur the added complexity and cost of a second CD player? When I asked BMW, they wouldn't say.

Inefficient Control

To enter an address for GPS navigation, the driver needed to use the controller to scroll though the alphabet to highlight and select each letter in turn. As a reviewer in *Automobile* magazine wrote, "It took longer for me to program the BMW's navigation system than in any vehicle I've tested!"[22] The controller dial was simply too inefficient a control for such a task, especially compared to touchscreens.

Graphic Design

When compared to the state of the art in other media, the on-screen graphic design was low quality, with extraneous labels and color coding, odd tabular data alignment, cryptic icons, and so on. I suspect it adversely affected usability, and—as research suggests—it probably negatively influenced the system's perceived credibility.[23]

Independent Testing

In 2005 researchers in Sweden tested the usability of iDrive compared to Audi's similar MMI system and Jaguar's touchscreen system, all of which were new designs trying to integrate multiple communication and entertainment functions.

They asked drivers to perform a set of tasks and recorded the time each task required (Figure 2.6). Drivers new to the systems performed tasks more slowly with the BMW and Audi systems, perhaps explaining the initial reactions of frustration that were common. The Swedish researchers reported, "For naive users a visual touchscreen seems to be the easiest, while an integrated rotary switch seems to be the most difficult one to operate."[24]

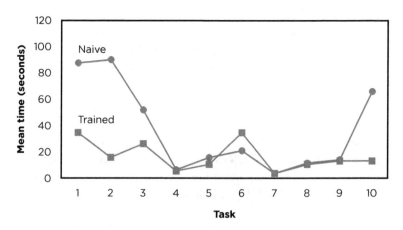

FIGURE 2.6
For people unfamiliar with iDrive ("Naive"), the time required to perform simple tasks, such as selecting a radio station preset (Task 2), was exceedingly long.

The researchers found that for both new and experienced drivers, the majority of usability problems had "a lot to do with the graphical interaction solutions and less to do with the actual manual interaction principle." [25] In other words, they found that the problems were largely caused by the on-screen design and didn't depend on whether the system used a rotary knob or a touchscreen. One confusing example from the test can be seen in Figure 2.7, the iDrive radio station preset display. In some ways it looks like a traditional analog radio dial with preset radio buttons laid on top of it in cascading rows. I imagine the cascade was used to save horizontal space for the station frequencies, but the result doesn't fit the conceptual models of traditional systems.

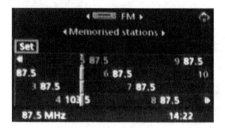

FIGURE 2.7

The early iDrive radio station preset listing was a confusing mash-up of traditional analog radio dials and preset radio buttons.

Product Evolution

I contacted BMW to ask about the design process that resulted in iDrive, but no one there would answer my questions. The company has never made any public statement admitting even the smallest shortcomings of iDrive. But since 2002 BMW has released several changes to iDrive. It decided to keep the essential iDrive concept of the controller and screen-based menus but gradually changed the design.

To revamp the system, the design process included research with 500 representative test participants in four locations in America, Asia, and Europe. It tested at varying levels of fidelity, using driving simulators, cockpit models, and two cars equipped with prototypes of a new design. To produce the new systems, BMW sourced the software and the controller from new suppliers.

The controller dial was made taller with a texture around the outside making it easier to hold and grip. The dial was changed from silver to black with high-contrast white arrows explicitly indicating the directions to tilt it. The tilting was reduced from eight directions to four. The haptic feedback was removed.

Perhaps the most radical change was the inclusion of more physical buttons to complement the controller. Originally, there was one small button behind the controller to return to the on-screen menu and another to activate voice control. Later that grew to seven buttons dedicated to making navigating the on-screen choices easier. Four buttons jumped directly to the most commonly used functions: Radio, CD, Telephone, and Navigation. The other three buttons provided quick navigation to go back one screen, to the main menu, and to the options screen (Figure 2.8).

FIGURE 2.8
The revised iDrive controller, now surrounded by seven buttons.

Additionally, eight programmable memory buttons were located on the dashboard (Figure 2.9). These could be used to directly access anything from radio stations to navigation points.

FIGURE 2.9
Eight memory buttons on a 2013 BMW.

The on-screen presentation underwent a complete redesign. The menus were presented as clear lists as Audi did with its MMI system (and not unlike Apple's iPod). With an option to split the screen, a menu and its submenu could be shown simultaneously. So although the menus were still categorized by topic, they could be navigated more quickly. The screen itself grew from 6.6 inches to 10.2 inches. The quality of the graphic design improved overall, with a clearer typeface, spelled-out words, and the removal of extraneous informational clutter (Figure 2.10). For a video overview of the redesigned iDrive, go to http://rfld.me/X909jC.

Overall the system responded more quickly, without the seconds-long delays common in the first version. But some tasks, such as spelling a street name in the navigation, were still awkward because they still relied on turning the controller.

FIGURE 2.10
The revised iDrive LCD display.

The reaction from customers and the media to later generations of iDrive was significantly more positive. However, although there were improvements, it was still the same essential design with the same essential learning curve. This fact was reflected in more recent reviews:

> Perhaps it's quite good to those who spent lots of time with the truly horrid first generation, but for someone who's hardly ever used it at all, it's still a bit obtuse. . . . The climate and entertainment sections, previously virtuoso confusers, received the most content changes, though operators still will need to scrutinize the owner's manual more than once to master the system.
>
> —David Zenlea, *Automobile*[26]

> For all of its simplification and refinement over the years, many people still find iDrive too complex for their tastes.
>
> —*Winding Road*[27]

> Despite dramatic improvements, the multi-function menu-driven "iDrive" controller still takes concentration. Though now augmented with numerous hard keys, it takes a great deal of fiddling with the iDrive knob while watching its central monitor screen to manipulate various audio, navigation, and cell-phone activities. Some will like the fact that you can program the navigation system while driving, but others will realize that doing so tempts fate.
>
> —*Consumer Reports*[28]

In the intervening years, other automakers rolled out integrated systems of their own, and the iDrive was judged not only against earlier versions of itself but also against the competition:

> The iDrive-style controller [in the Hyundai Genesis] is much more intuitive and easier to use than iDrive itself.
>
> —Joe DeMatio, *Automobile*[29]

> [Ford's] Sync beats iDrive.
>
> —*Motor Trend*[30]

So far, I've found iDrive to be vastly improved. . . . I'll also
admit that the new and improved iDrive is not particularly
groundbreaking—Audi, Honda/Acura, Nissan/Infiniti, have
been continually improving their systems in the time it has
taken BMW to get [to] this point. I'd say iDrive still fails to
beat them in a few ways.

—*Motor Trend*[31]

It was enlightening to fall into this [Mercedes] directly after
spending a couple of hours in the Audi and the BMW. It was a
physical and mental relief. The oldest car in our group of four,
the Mercedes S-class is comforting and familiar. The seats
are instantly and easily adjustable. The controls are all where
you expect them to be and work in ways that are familiar to
anyone who has ever driven a modern car. . . . Let us pray . . .
that Mercedes-Benz will resist any notion of following BMW
into the iDrive jungle.

—*Automobile*[32]

Quantitative Results

J.D. Power and Associates publishes an annual ranking of automakers
by initial quality. It acquires this data by asking customers what defects
they found in the cars they owned. In 2005 BMW ranked very highly—
third best out of 37 automakers, with 95 defects per 100 cars. But in 2006
J.D. Power changed the criteria of its initial quality study to ask customers not only about defects but also about design problems. BMW fell
from 3rd to 26th position, with 142 defects and design problems per 100
cars. The top "most troublesome design failure problem" identified by
BMW drivers in 2006 was the "difficult to use" and "poorly located" front
audio and entertainment system.[33]

Between 2002 and 2008, sales of the 7 series in the United States declined
by almost half—from more than 20,000 per year to 12,276—and have not
recovered since (Figure 2.11).[34]

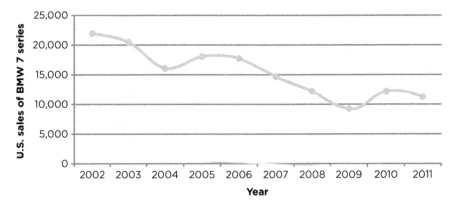

FIGURE 2.11

U.S. sales of the BMW 7 series, 2002–2011. Sales were noticeably slumping even before the economic downturn in late 2008.

Google Wave

Next is a story about Google. BMW and Google are very different companies but these two stories share many similarities. In the end, it was Google's corporate culture that led it to the opposite conclusion about how to address a bad product experience.

A Noble Beginning

Like BMW's iDrive, Google Wave was preceded by decades of established technology that people used and understood, but that had become complicated, disconnected, and inefficient. In the case of Wave, the technology was online communication for collaboration. To appreciate the problem, consider what people commonly use now to communicate with others online: Chat is used for real-time text. E-mail is used to send messages asynchronously with file attachments. Forums are used for threaded conversations. Wikis or browser-based online document services such as Google Docs are used for shared document editing. And every time some new feature is needed, customers must find new and different software rather than having a way to add that function to what they already use.

Like the proliferating buttons on an automotive dashboard, there should be a way to combine this disparate software into one coherent service to accomplish more work more quickly with less complexity. Google Wave was this service, designed to use a Web browser to help people communicate in new ways.

The Design

Essentially, a "wave" was a page on the Web where multiple people could add and edit text and multimedia content in real time.

By default the Google Wave screen had four panels (Figure 2.12). In the middle was the Search panel that displayed a list of waves matching search criteria.

FIGURE 2.12

Google Wave's main screen. In the middle is the Search panel, shown here displaying all waves in the Inbox. When a wave is selected, as with the Snapshots! wave shown here, it's displayed in the Wave panel on the right.

When someone started a new wave, it was displayed in the Wave panel on the right. They could type a message in that panel and then select people to share it with from the Contacts panel on the lower left. When someone wanted to contribute to the wave, he or she could reply and leave a new message below the last message, or double-click anywhere in the wave to edit any content, even if someone else created the content. Everyone in a wave could edit content at the same time, and each person could see the other members' edits as they typed (Figure 2.13). Wave could autocorrect misspellings and auto-translate in real time. To see which edits happened when, a person could click the Playback button and watch the edits happen one by one. And because this all happened in a Web browser, virtually any kind of content could be added to a wave, such as images, videos, maps, and even applications. For example, a Yes/No/Maybe application could be added to ask friends a question and let them answer with a single click (Figure 2.14).

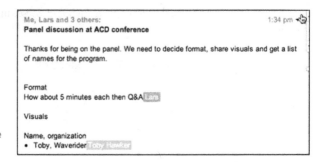

FIGURE 2.13
Detail of the Wave panel showing the names of other people editing the wave.

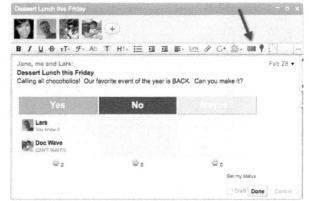

FIGURE 2.14
Detail of the Wave panel showing the Yes/No/Maybe application.

To find a wave, a term could be typed into the box at the top of the Search panel or a link could be selected from the Navigation panel at the upper left.

Wave contained a great deal of interesting technology. An entire wave could be embedded into another website, just like YouTube videos. Images and files could be dragged and dropped into a wave instead of having to attach them. And the spellcheck had some understanding of grammar, so it could differentiate between "to" and "too" or "their" and "they're." (For a demonstration, watch the Getting Started with Google Wave video at http://rfld.me/WCJUKs.)

Wave had the potential to change the way people collaborate online. It even had the potential to replace some old but vital technologies such as e-mail. I'm personally disappointed that Wave didn't evolve and survive because it could have been enormously useful, but the reasons for its failure are clear.

The Customer Experience

Google had built an impressive track record of online innovation from their beginnings as a search engine to their expansion into new areas such as online advertising and e-mail. It would not have been unreasonable to call Google the most innovative Internet company in the world. So when Wave was announced in May 2009, widespread excitement ensued, even though no one was sure exactly what Wave was. Adding to the anticipation was Google's use of an invitation system to limit the number of people using Wave so that an onslaught of visitors wouldn't overload their systems.

In September 2009 Google sent out the first round of invitations to 100,000 people. Some people adopted Wave quickly and enthusiastically, finding novel ways to collaborate with others. But for many people, Wave was confusing, and it confused on multiple levels.

First there was confusion around how to access it. Google's invite-only testing periods had worked successfully in the past with products like Gmail, but Wave could only be used with others on Wave. If you received an invitation from Google, you could also invite eight friends (Figure 2.15), but those friends couldn't invite anyone. If the friends or colleagues you wanted to collaborate with didn't have an invitation, then Wave was reduced to a fancy electronic notebook.

FIGURE 2.15
Sending others an invitation
to join Wave.

Next, the layout was new, unfamiliar, and with four panels, a bit complex. To anyone who had used Gmail, the navigation, contacts, and search would look familiar, but otherwise the mash-up of contacts, messages, and documents was a daunting sight for many people.

The interaction was the most confusing. If your mental model of a wave was "waves are like e-mails, but they do more" and you were accustomed to e-mail interfaces like Gmail that offer robust search as the primary way of finding messages, the thought was that you could adapt to finding waves using search. Judging by questions in help forums, the biggest problem with this interaction was that people would lose waves. Someone would scroll down the list of waves and a wave that used to be there was now missing, often because they had recently entered a search term, narrowed the list of waves in the Search panel, and then forgotten they had done that.

By far the most fascinating and challenging aspect of interaction on Wave was the fact that anyone in a wave could edit any part of it, as on wikis. Although this was a powerful feature for collaboration, it also made tracking changes difficult. Again, if your mental model was "waves are like documents, but they do more" and you were accustomed to scanning documents from Microsoft Word with changes noted throughout, you could adapt to scanning waves for changes. But if you thought of waves as being like e-mails or forum conversations, looking for changes throughout a wave was a whole new behavior. The Wave designers included the helpful Playback feature to step through each change, but jumping from one part of a wave to another part that might have different participants and different content required a lot of cognitive work to repeatedly comprehend the new context, what was changed, and what each change meant in each new context. People do this now, switching among applications and content as they work, but at a much slower pace. Wave's intense context-switching was integral to the design, but it caused a lot of cognitive fatigue compared to what people were used to.

In conventional text chat with one other person, we sometimes experience the taking-turns problem—one of us types a response before the other person has finished their thought. Maybe a false assumption is made. A flurry of apologies or clarifications follows. Current chat applications try to help you avoid this by signaling to you when the other person is typing. In Wave, the taking-turns problem was amplified. Multiple people could be in a wave at the same time and could not only add messages but also edit content, any content, simultaneously. For the developers this was an awesomely powerful and sophisticated capability. But for most people, the conversational convention of politely waiting until someone else has finished speaking (or typing or editing) got trampled.

Wave was also confusing on a conceptual level. During the lifetime of a wave, the group of people who participated in the wave could grow and shrink. Some people had the expectation that, like a one-to-one chat session, there's a reasonable assumption of privacy. Wave made these people anxious about who would be able to see the content in the future and who could reply. The flip side of Wave's powerful, fluid collaboration was the unnerving worry about access privileges.

One early clue that Wave might be too confusing was that everyone had a different definition of Wave. Here are four definitions I came across:

> Google Wave is a real-time communication platform.
>
> —Ben Parr, Mashable[35]

> Google Wave is an integrated set of technologies.
>
> —Oliver Wrede, personal blog[36]

> A "wave" is equal parts conversation and document.
>
> —Lars Rasmussen,
> Google Wave software engineering manager[37]

> It's a hybrid of email, web chat, IM, and project management software.
>
> —Ben Parr, Mashable[38]

Yes, Wave was all of those things, and that's another reason it was so hard to comprehend.

Of course any new product that intends to innovate requires some learning, but if the product concept is too far beyond convention, it's probably too hard to understand. A classic interface design guideline is that any object that looks familiar should behave in a familiar way. Waves looked like e-mails and documents but didn't act like either of them.

Reactions

Wave generated extreme reactions from the public. The initial May 2009 announcement caused a few of Google's followers to admit they didn't understand it, but mostly it generated awesome anticipation. The media gushed about its potential and said it "drips with ambition" although some predicted a customer backlash (Figure 2.16). People were rabid for invitations, to the point of buying them on auction sites.

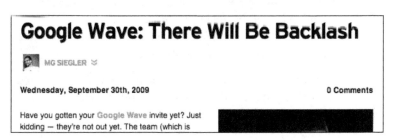

FIGURE 2.16
A story on the popular Techcrunch blog foresees the reaction to the highly anticipated product release.

In the months that followed, with many people still eagerly awaiting their invitations, those who had received invitations reported their experiences online. A few were still enthusiastic and committed to using it, but most complained loudly of usability problems. "Someone deleted content from my wave, why can't I undo that?" "My wave is a mess of replies, why can't I hide some content?" "Why can't I get a notification by email when a wave is updated?" Google officially called this time a "preview" period, and like any fledgling, complex, and popular system, it could be slow and unreliable at times.

Within days of receiving invitations, technology writers lashed out. Robert Scoble, the American blogger and technical evangelist, had this reaction:

> This service is way overhyped and as people start to use it they will realize it brings the worst of email and IM together: unproductively. . . .
>
> . . . [W]hen I look at my Google Wave page I see dozens of people all typing to me in real time. I don't know where to look and keeping up with this real time noise is less like email, which is like tennis (hit one ball at a time) and more like dodging a machine gun of tennis balls. Much more mentally challenging.[39]

Here is blogger Louis Gray:

> It can be a productivity sink. If you thought Twitter or Friend-
> Feed could chew up cycles, Wave takes it to another level. I
> had a wonderful chat or three last night, and it was a great
> tool for that. But there is no way I can possibly see every
> update on every wave, just like I can't see every comment on
> every FriendFeed thread. It can't replace e-mail for me in this
> case because with e-mail, it is assumed I read the messages.[40]

Even when it came to Google employees, presumably the people this
technology wouldn't confuse, usage was apparently moderate at best.
There are reports that engineering teams regularly used Wave as groupware, while others report it was seldom used: "By early 2010 it was still
considered novel, almost lampooning, to create a group Wave. They were
usually introduced with some lighthearted caveat like 'That's right, this
is a WAVE.'"[41]

In October 2009, while still in the limited preview release, Wave was
parodied online by EasierToUnderstandThanWave.com, which let visitors vote on which was easier to understand, Wave or one of a rotating
parade of obtuse and humorous comparisons, from metaphysics to
Sarah Palin (Figure 2.17). The popular sentiment was clear.

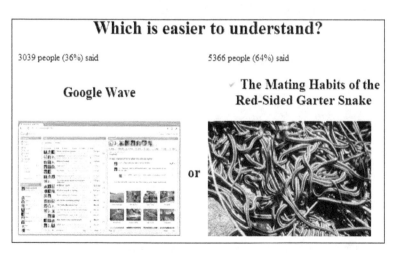

FIGURE 2.17
One comparison from EasierToUnderstandThanWave.com.

A Race to the Stoplight

Google had spent much of 2009 courting the developer community, and over the course of 2009 and 2010 third-party developers created dozens of Wave-compatible applications. Google released many more invitations in December 2009. In 2010 they rolled out more features and fixed some of the functional problems such as the inability to restore deleted content and the lack of e-mail notifications of updates. But by that time it was too late to make fundamental changes in the design. Wave had been under development for years and the applications that the development partners had built relied on the way Wave was designed.

Google opened Wave to the public in May 2010, but by then Wave's reputation as a confusing product had stuck, and the excitement to try it had faded. The lead developer said fewer than one million people actively used Wave, a small number by Google's standards. The team had grown so large it became a significant expense and focus for the company. In August 2010, less than a year after the first invitations were sent, Google announced they would close Wave, saying, "Wave has not seen the user adoption we would have liked"[42] (Figure 2.18).

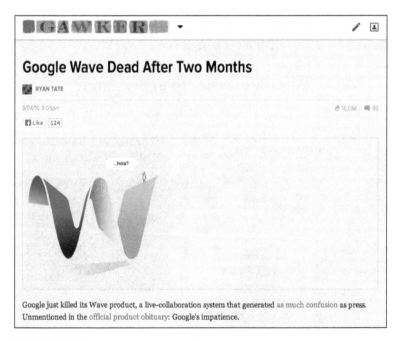

FIGURE 2.18
A story on the Gawker blog emphasizes how little time Wave had to prove itself.

Lessons

In the early 2000s, Bob Lutz, a former executive of Chrysler, Ford, BMW, and General Motors, was reported to have said, "The automotive technology that is now possible has surpassed what is desirable." Not long after hearing this, in 2012, I saw a full-page ad in the *New York Times* for Audi's MMI system with the headline, "People have landed on the moon with less technology at their fingertips." Indeed.

From the evidence it seems that both iDrive and Wave began not with customer experience goals but with technology goals, throwing out what came before in order to usher in a grand unified system. You can hear this in the language the companies used to introduce the systems:

> The Control Center has been designed to avoid the unnecessary complexity created by an extended number of switches and controls.
>
> —BMW 2002 745i/745Li Owner's Manual[43]

> Two of the most spectacular successes in digital communication, e-mail and instant messaging, were originally designed in the '60s to imitate analog formats—email mimicked snail mail, and IM mimicked phone calls. Since then, so many different forms of communication had been invented—blogs, wikis, collaborative documents, etc.—and computers and networks had dramatically improved. So Jens proposed a new communications model that presumed all these advances as a starting point, and I was immediately sold.
>
> —Lars Rasmussen,
> Google Wave software engineering manager[44]

How did these two companies, both with a track record of great customer experiences, become blinded by overwrought technology?

Cultural Differences

As an American driver, I have the typical fascination with German Autobahns, where some sections have no speed limits and where you can press your accelerator all the way down and drive truly fast, legally. The first time I had the opportunity to drive through Germany I discovered the reality of the Autobahn: For the first minute or so, speeding down the Autobahn was a thrill, moving into the left lane and pushing my rental car as fast as it would go. But before long I would see headlights in my rear-view mirror, the headlights of a luxury or sports car bearing down on me at an unbelievable speed. If I didn't have an empty space to my right to get out of the left lane, I suddenly found myself in a dangerous situation.

How can Germans drive this fast without catastrophic accidents occurring every day? To earn a driver's license in Germany requires taking 14 theory classes and 12 driving lessons at a driving school over the course of three months at a cost of more than 1,000 euros. German drivers are better trained than American drivers, and they take driving more seriously. The rate of motor vehicle fatalities in Germany is *half* of that in the United States.[45]

A German BMW driver is probably more likely to sit in a parked car for an hour, read the manual, and properly learn how to operate iDrive. Americans just get behind the wheel and go, hence the American frustration with iDrive. The German automotive media acknowledged iDrive was not easy, but did not critique it with the same venom as their American counterparts.[46]

Similarly, the Google engineers and employees who created and vetted Wave were more computer literate than the vast majority of their customers.

Customers Overlook Flaws

We know that BMW 7 series sales declined. But if iDrive was so bad, why did some people keep buying the cars? One reason could be that buyers, especially early in the iDrive product cycle, simply didn't experience iDrive until after buying the car. One survey found that a surprising number of people don't test-drive a car before buying it: 11.4 percent of U.S. buyers and 26 percent of Canadian buyers.[47]

For the rest, the overall experience of driving a BMW is so good flaws are often overlooked. I know from having owned a BMW (pre-iDrive) that the experience is qualitatively better than in other cars because BMW uses technology effectively. The engines are smooth. The gear shifters are satisfying. The seats are comfortable. The cars turn a corner with utter competence, feeling like one solid piece of forged metal. Even the optics of the windshield glass look much clearer and glare-free than in other cars.

Wave, too, was capable of amazing tasks, but for most people the frustration outweighed the benefits. If people had needed to occasionally use

Wave as part of using Google, as people use iDrive as part of driving a BMW, maybe they would have tolerated Wave. But because Wave was a separate application, people weren't tempted to overlook its flaws.

Companies Overlook Flaws

BMW boasts a long history of innovation and high performance. The company was the first to use xenon headlights, the first European car manufacturer to offer an integrated satellite navigation screen, and the first European manufacturer to offer a heads-up display. They have raced their cars and motorcycles with success since the 1920s. For close to 100 years they have produced vehicles at the leading edge of performance and have good reason to believe they are one of the best auto manufacturers in the world. But too much confidence can become hubris.

As Frank Markus at *Motor Trend* noted in a 2005 review of the 7 series,[48]

> I noticed one fatal flaw [with iDrive]. . . . Anyone wearing polarized sunglasses would see a blank screen.
>
> I mentioned the problem to the engineers, expecting to hear that our screens were prototypes. Instead they said they knew of the issue and saw no need to make any changes. Huh? People can't see your new gizmo, and you think that's okay?! Ja.
>
> The screen was quietly changed, but the utter refusal to admit there might be a problem smacked of hubris.

Later in the same piece Markus wrote:

> At the recent launch of the 2006 7 Series, BMW brass delighted in rubbing the gathered media's collective nose in these statistics, telling us again and again how this is the most successful 7 Series ever and how Audi's MMI knob and other systems like it validate the iDrive concept. . . . So did we pundits all get it wrong?
>
> Indeed this 7 is a global best-seller, thanks to BMW's expansion into new markets. But in the U.S., sales have declined precipitously to 16,155 in 2004—a level below all but the first and last years of the previous car. Maybe after two years, lessees longed for . . . normal radio buttons and walked away from their 7s.

BMW's propaganda isn't unusual in the automotive industry. Auto companies rarely admit failure even if everyone else knows it. But the confident, independent nature of BMW is a thing apart. *Motor Trend*'s editor, Edward Loh, points out that, "As one of the smaller auto manufacturers in the world, BMW thinks very differently about the fundamentals of the car."[49] You could hear that difference made explicit in the 2006 "Company of Ideas" advertising campaign, in which BMW proudly proclaimed that its independent corporate identity helps creativity thrive, which in turn allows it to "keep turning convention on its ear."[50] This approach works most of the time, but not always.

Google's culture comes across as more sincere and humble, though it is not without some hubris of its own. The Wave product concept should have been tested early with customers because it was so radical, and yet Google waited until too much was built to expose the product to criticism. According to Lars Rasmussen, Wave co-founder and software engineering manager, "After months holed up in a conference room in the Sydney office, our five-person 'startup' team emerged with a prototype. And now, after more than two years of expanding our ideas, our team, and technology, we're very eager to return and see what the world might think."[51]

I could not get an official response from Google commenting on the Wave design process, but from the ex-Google employees I spoke to it seems the Wave team was allowed to work outside the company's usual product development process. At the time, Google would typically release a new product in the Google Labs area of their website, where early adopters could try it and report problems, allowing Google developers to refine the product before a wider public release. Google didn't do that in this case, and I've heard two possible factors to explain why. One is that Wave was built by the people who built Google Maps, one of the company's most impressive and successful products, so the team was given a lot of freedom to follow their own process. Another is that the team was located in Australia, far from the everyday control of the corporate office in California.

By the time Google got the product into customers' hands, the company would have had to undo years of development to fix the problems they found. Although the interaction design was confusing and the rollout schedule precluded the opportunity to fix major problems once they were found, the failure to test the product early in the development cycle was the key, fatal error of the Wave project.

Google generally didn't acknowledge the outcry of confusion, but it did admit that people experienced problems. Results from a customer survey published on their blog in November 2009 revealed, for example, that the top complaint, "My friends/contacts don't have accounts," was twice as prevalent as the next most common complaint, "It's too slow." But Google did stop short of divulging just how many complaints they received.[52]

FIGURE 2.19
Google CEO Eric Schmidt, left, explains to reporters the decision to close Google Wave.

Though the cases of BMW iDrive and Google Wave share many similarities, what sets Google apart is how it treated its failure. Rather than iterate on the design for years, letting customers suffer through a fundamentally flawed concept that was costing a lot of money to develop, the company killed it. Google CEO Eric Schmidt did admit that Wave failed (Figure 2.19), albeit in roundabout corporate-speak:

> We liked the UI. And we liked a lot of the features. But it didn't get enough traction. . . .
>
> We try things. Remember, we celebrate our failures. This is a company where it's absolutely okay to try something that's very hard, have it not be successful, then take the learning from that and apply it to something new.[53]

The Competition

BMW did not plunge alone into the waters of experimental telematics; others had usability challenges as well, albeit to a lesser extent. When the aforementioned COMAND system from Mercedes was launched, it was hardly much better than iDrive. Although Mercedes improved COMAND over the years, in 2012 both drivers and automotive journalists were still complaining about the long time needed to learn their way around the hierarchical menus.

Volkswagen confounded owners with the on-screen menus in the 2004 VW Phaeton. Ford released the praiseworthy Sync system only to spoil it by layering the flawed MyTouch touchscreen on top. Jaguar's touchscreen was woefully underpowered and paused disconcertingly after each press of a finger.

A decade after the introduction of iDrive, automakers are still confusing their customers when mixing software and hardware controls. In a review of the 2012 Dodge Charger, Ezra Dyer wrote,

> That touch screen also controls the seat heaters, a fact I realized after about 20 minutes behind the wheel of a Charger R/T. I pushed a button on the console adorned with a heating and cooling icon, then sat wondering why my seat was still cold but my Diet Coke in the cupholder was getting warmer by the minute. While I appreciate heated drinks, I might suggest that the hard button would be better devoted to the human holder than the beverage holder.[54]

In Google's case, there was no competition. Though some products tried to integrate chat, e-mail, and multimedia, nothing else had the Web technology sophistication of Google Wave.

The Wider Ramifications

After years of subpar usability of integrated technology inside the automobile, the U.S. government began to issue warnings. In February 2012 the National Highway Traffic Safety Administration published a 131-page document detailing guidelines for "secondary tasks using original equipment," the kind of tasks not required to drive the car that were handled by automakers' systems like iDrive.[55] The report cites analysis that "17 percent of all police-reported crashes involved some type of driver distraction in 2010" and that 26,000 accidents were caused by distraction from "a device/control integral to the vehicle," such as a navigation or infotainment system (Table 2.1). Although the overall number of accidents declined during this period, the accidents related to integrated control devices like iDrive rose. The report includes guidelines on the placement of controls, viewing angles, a test protocol, criteria for selecting human test subjects, and much more.[56]

TABLE 2.1 POLICE REPORTED CRASHES AND CRASHES INVOLVING DISTRACTION, 2006–2010

Year	Number of police-reported crashes	Police-reported crashes involving a distracted driver	Distraction-related crashes involving an integrated control/device*	Distraction-related crashes involving an electronic device*
2006	5,964,000	1,019,000 (17%)	18,000 (2%)	24,000 (2%)
2007	6,016,000	1,001,000 (17%)	23,000 (2%)	48,000 (5%)
2008	5,801,000	967,000 (17%)	21,000 (2%)	48,000 (5%)
2009	5,498,000	957,000 (17%)	22,000 (2%)	46,000 (5%)
2010	5,409,000	899,000 (17%)	26,000 (3%)	47,000 (5%)

* The categories for Integrated Control/Device and Electronic Device are not mutually exclusive. Therefore the data cannot be added or combined in any manner.

Source: National Highway Traffic Safety Administration, "Visual Manual-NHTSA Driver Distraction Guidelines for In-Vehicle Electronic Devices," February 24, 2012, www.federalregister.gov /articles/2012/02/24/2012-4017/visual-manual-nhtsa-driver-distraction-guidelines-for-in -vehicle-electronic-devices#p-537.

Google Wave was shut down before inflicting undue damage on its customers. But judging from other case studies in this book, we know that's not always the case. Designers of consumer software generally enjoy a regulation-free work environment, unlike the automotive industry. But as online services increasingly become a vital part of our everyday lives, one wonders if government regulations that are commonplace for automobiles will become similarly commonplace for all digital services.

Summary

BMW iDrive

What it is: BMW's iDrive is a computer system used to control audio, navigation, climate, and other secondary functions in many BMW cars. Since its release in 2002, millions of people have driven with iDrive. BMW's investment includes system development over more than 10 years.

Summary continues on next page

Summary (continued)

Why the experience failed: A radical departure from familiar vehicle controls, the initial versions of iDrive had several design flaws, and people experienced enormous frustration using it. Since iDrive launched it has been widely criticized in the media. BMW received lower rankings for quality because of iDrive, and sales of the high-priced 7 series cars have fallen significantly in the United States since the introduction of iDrive.

The underlying cause: BMW launched a radically designed integrated electronics system, an area outside of their traditional range of expertise, and one in which all automakers struggle. The original concept was conceived as an advance in technology, not of the customer's experience. The initial iDrive was probably not tested sufficiently, possibly due to BMW's corporate overconfidence. Since its original release, BMW has significantly redesigned iDrive.

The lesson: Radically new concepts can lead to huge breakthroughs or huge failures, so the courage to pursue a bold concept must be tempered by an appropriate risk management plan, particularly a lot of product testing of the basic design concept.

Google Wave

What it was: Google Wave was an online, real-time, collaborative service for creating documents. Google invested about three years of development and, at launch, 50 developers were working on Wave.

Why the experience failed: The product concept and interaction design were too confusing and cognitively intense.

The underlying cause: Wave was entirely in Google's area of expertise, and Google had an effective process for testing new services. But Google may have abandoned its usual discipline because the team leaders had a hugely successful track record and the team was located in another office remote from corporate headquarters. Like BMW's iDrive, Google Wave was conceived as an advance in technology, not of the customer's experience. Because third-party developers received early access to Wave and built extensions to it, the public launch process didn't allow for making fundamental improvements. The service attracted fewer than a million people, low by Google's standards, and after being available to the public for only two and a half months, Google announced it would shut down the service.

The lesson: If you have a successful product-testing process in place, follow it every time. If you're building a platform that requires third-party developer support, it's even more important to test with customers before attracting developers.

Get the Experience Right

It doesn't matter how many times I have to click, as long as each click is a mindless, unambiguous choice.

—Steve Krug[1]

By the mid-2000s the process for signing in to a website account had reached an ad hoc standard: remember and type in a username and password. Having to remember all those usernames and passwords is difficult, but the concept is well understood. OpenID tried to address the problem people had with remembering all of their credentials.

But OpenID arrived at a time when the Internet was evolving into a more experiential medium. Before the World Wide Web, the Internet was more functional and mostly consisted of command-line or menu-driven interfaces. After the Web, rich graphics, sound, and interaction engaged us more fully, and our expectations for how easy technology should be to use rose accordingly.

As first invented, OpenID was clever technology that was well suited for the narrow, technical audience it was originally designed for. But the attempt to turn it into a mainstream standard without first subjecting it to a proper design process sent OpenID out of step with the current expectations of usability.

OpenID

In July 2008 a team at Yahoo! ran a series of tests on the OpenID method for signing in to a website, a method used by their own sites and thousands of others for the preceding two years, and found to their surprise that people didn't understand what OpenID was or how to access it, much less how to use it (Figure 3.1).[2] A technology evangelist on the team confessed, "Observing these tests was more than a bit frustrating for the Yahoo! OpenID team, and the test subjects may have been distracted by the sounds of the groans and head-pounding coming from the other side of the one-way mirror. Certainly there is a lot of work to be done on the OpenID UX front."[3]

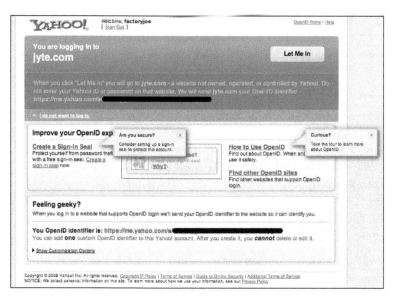

FIGURE 3.1

One type of screen used in Yahoo!'s OpenID usability test.

History

Around 2005 the Internet technology community foresaw a problem that would arise with the exploding number of applications stored not on people's computers but over a network. If every application separately stored usernames and passwords for every customer, a host of usability, security, and data management problems would result. For example, the average person might be expected to remember dozens of name and password combinations to access vital information throughout the day.

Large sites such as Yahoo! developed their own proprietary methods to centralize sign-in so their customers could use one name and password across diverse services, such as shopping and e-mail. Similarly, Brad Fitzpatrick at LiveJournal wanted to allow readers to sign in to LiveJournal once and then be able to comment on any of the millions of LiveJournal blogs. So he invented Yadis, which stood for "Yet another distributed identity system." The technology community perceived a potential mess of competing technologies and realized there should be one universal standard. Support rallied around Yadis because it was the most simple and had proved itself by working on LiveJournal. Gradually, more volunteers and companies collaborated on improving the technology, making it operate on different systems and with different programming languages. Yadis was renamed OpenID, and in June 2007 the nonprofit OpenID Foundation was formed to provide formal support.

The Design

One goal of OpenID was to simplify the task of signing in to many different websites by replacing the process with OpenID's method. As designed in version 1.0, the customer would start by getting an OpenID through a third-party provider. After completing a registration form, the customer would be given a personalized uniform resource identifier (URI), such as http://myOpenIDprovider.com/VictorLombardi. This takes a bit of work, but once I have my OpenID, I can use it across multiple sites without registering on each one.

You can watch a video demonstration of how it worked at http://rfld.me/WCK18D.

To sign in to a site that accepts OpenID, such as Yahoo! Mail, I simply type in my URI instead of a name and password (Figure 3.2). It's as simple as that. Behind the scenes Yahoo! Mail checks with my OpenID provider to see if I'm signed in there from the same computer. If so, Yahoo! Mail let's me in. The mechanics behind the scenes are fast and smooth.

FIGURE 3.2
A typical OpenID sign-in form.

As a concept, OpenID is elegant and promising, and it is easy to understand why large companies such as Microsoft, AOL, and Symantec said they would use it on their sites. Smaller website producers signed up because OpenID offered the ability to outsource registration, sign-in, and password recovery functions, along with the accompanying customer service. And many smart, prominent technologists who advocate for open standards were recommending OpenID, as were technology news outlets such as ZDNet.

Individuals signed up assuming OpenID must be a better way because so many websites offered it. If it worked as hoped, the outcome of having one way to sign in to many services would be great. But ultimately people don't know if the experience is good until they experience it.

The Experience

Unfortunately, the experience of using OpenID fell far short of what was intended.

To start with, getting an OpenID from a provider wasn't a standardized process. Each provider could use a sign-up form of their own design. For example, to get an OpenID I followed a link to VeriSign Labs at https://pip.verisignlabs.com. When I arrived there, I saw branding for another company, Symantec, for a service called the Personal Identity Portal, also known as PIP (Figure 3.3). For a service that should make me feel secure, I'm already feeling a bit disoriented and confused, and I haven't even signed up yet. Only when I read closely did I see that it mentions OpenID.

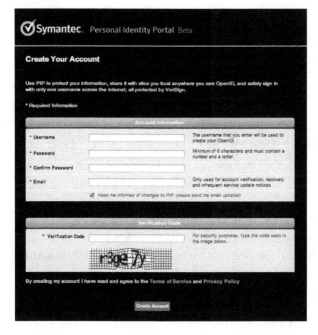

FIGURE 3.3
The VeriSign Labs/
Symantec Personal
Identity Portal, actually
an OpenID registration
form in disguise.

Once I completed this form I received my OpenID. It could be days or weeks before I came across a site where I can use it, and by then I may have forgotten my URI. Remembering a URI that can only be used on some websites that support OpenID is harder than remembering my own e-mail address or a username that I use multiple times a day.

Look back at Figure 3.2 and notice that the OpenID form doesn't indicate what I am supposed to type. A username? An e-mail address? A password? The OpenID sign-in form was also not standard and often lacked simple labeling to help people remember what their OpenID looked like. If it had been a while since I used my OpenID, I might have forgotten it was a URI. For all the shortcomings of usernames and passwords, the forms are usually labeled well and people understand how to use them.

If all OpenID providers used the same URI format, people might become accustomed to the standard over time. But each provider chose how they wanted to format the URI. For example:

- http://claimid.com/yourname

- http://yourname.signon.com

- https://me.yahoo.com/yourname[4]

If I forgot my URI I had to go to the provider's site to recover it, which also required remembering which provider I used (VeriSign Labs/Symantec) to get my OpenID. That's much more difficult cognitively than the convention, which is to just look around on the page and find the "Forget your username or password?" link to recover or reset a username or password. OpenID expected people to remember both their URI and the provider they used to get the URI. As the classic usability guideline tells us, recognition of something you can see is easier than recalling something from memory.[5]

Let's say I'm trying to sign in to Yahoo! Mail and I enter my OpenID URI but I wasn't signed in to the provider site (the Personal Identity Portal, or PIP). Yahoo! Mail would redirect me there so I could enter my name and password for PIP, and then redirect me back to Yahoo! Mail. The technical "handshake" going on behind the scenes is impressive when it works, but using it gives me the unsettling experience of being pushed away from the website I was trying to access. And if I forgot my username and password, I had to use my *provider's* (PIP's) "Forget your username or password?" function. The method for recovering usernames and passwords is also nonstandard across OpenID providers, and again might not even mention OpenID anywhere on the screen (Figure 3.4).

Even when I learned how to use OpenID to sign in on one website, I wasn't guaranteed to know how to use it on other sites because the design varied across sites. The technology under the hood was standard, but how that technology was presented to me was not (Figures 3.5, 3.6, and 3.7).

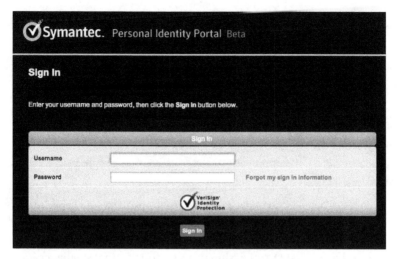

FIGURE 3.4

If I try to use my OpenID and I'm not signed in to my OpenID provider, I'm redirected there to sign in. Each provider uses a unique
design that may not even mention OpenID.

FIGURE 3.5

To type in my OpenID URI on Stack-
Exchange, I need to first click "More
OpenID options."

FIGURE 3.6

Twitterfeed tried to make signing in
easier by displaying a list of OpenID
providers and, once one was selected,
prefilling the URI format. This could
be helpful, as long as visitors recognized their OpenID provider's name
and/or logo.

FIGURE 3.7
A generic OpenID
sign-in form with
another unique design.

Even those people who understood and used OpenID would experience barriers due to the open and decentralized nature of the technology. OpenID providers sometimes had service outages or bugs, making it impossible to sign in to other sites using OpenID. Several smaller providers, such as Technorati and Vidoop, ceased operations, essentially making all the URIs they created obsolete.

Google conducted their own usability testing of OpenID and reported that people found it "confusing."[6]

MySpace tested it as well, and found that test participants were certainly enthusiastic about some aspects of OpenID:

- "They love the idea of having an ID that allows them to remember just one set of login credentials across the web."

- "More frequent MySpace users were enthusiastic about using their MySpace accounts as a 'parent' account."[7]

Unfortunately they encountered the same confusion as others:

- "[They] expected their MySpace information to automatically update the 3rd party account."

- "The notion of using a URL to sign in to a website baffles them."

- "Security concerns were high, particularly once users learned that the OpenID is simply their public MySpace URL."

Reactions

The experience of using OpenID received almost universal scorn. The Yahoo!, Google, and MySpace tests served to confirm what everyone knew anecdotally—that "the user experience of logging in with OpenID is worse than just signing up for another account."[8] In January 2011, the Web application company 37Signals announced that they would discontinue support for OpenID:

> We first jumped on the OpenID bandwagon back in 2007 when it was seen as a promising way to make logging into websites simpler. What we've learned over the past three years is that it didn't actually make anything any simpler for the vast majority of our customers. Instead it just made things harder. . . . OpenID has been a burden on support since the day it was launched.[9]

Rob Conery, co-founder of Tekpub.com, penned an entire article on the difficulty he experienced as a developer in implementing OpenID so it would work well for customers. Here's the analogy he offered to illustrate part of his experience:

> Let me just preface this by saying of all the failure points in your business—you really don't want the door to be locked while you stand behind the counter waiting for business. No, let me rephrase that: you don't want the door jammed shut, completely unopenable while your customers wait outside— irate that you won't let them in.[10]

Yishan Wong, the CEO of Reddit, offered this analogy:

> It is like saying to people, "Hey, I notice you have a lot of keys on your keyring. Wouldn't it be more convenient if you could unify them all so you wouldn't have to carry all those keys? (sounding pretty okay here so far . . .) All right, here, instead of using those keys, you should take this extremely convoluted and foreign-looking mobile phone, into which you have to insert all of your keys, type in a special password, and then oh, well, it works on most locks but not all of them, so you'll only be able to replace some of your keys with it, so now you should carry this new weird mobile phone on your keyring too. Also, it doesn't work as a phone. And it has other companies' brand names printed all over it. And it calls one of those companies whenever you use it."[11]

Competition

In December 2008 Facebook released Facebook Connect and the following April saw the release of Sign In with Twitter; both promised to help people sign in to sites around the Web, and both offered a much smoother experience. They used another technology called OAuth that works as part of the plumbing between sites rather than something people see. For example, the Vimeo website has the standard "Log in with Facebook" button (Figure 3.8).

FIGURE 3.8

Vimeo, the video-sharing website, offers the ability to "Log in with Facebook" using Facebook Connect.

Once I click on that button, a "Request for Permission" pop-up window appears with information telling me which pieces of information from Facebook will be shared (Figure 3.9). If I'm already signed in to Facebook, as are many of the hundreds of millions of regular Facebook visitors, I can click "Allow" or "Don't Allow." Because a pop-up window is used, Facebook avoids that unsettling feeling of leaving the site I was trying to sign in to.

If I'm not signed in to Facebook, I am prompted for my Facebook username and password before seeing the Request for Permission screen. Although the Facebook Connect method also requires this additional step, presumably more people know their Facebook credentials than their credentials for an OpenID provider.

There are times when this flow becomes even simpler. I can sign in to a service using Sign In with Twitter only to identify myself and not to connect it to Twitter, such as when commenting in a forum or on a blog. In this case, Sign In with Twitter can work with a single click (Figure 3.10).

FIGURE 3.9
Facebook Connect uses a pop-up window when requesting permission to transfer Facebook data to another site.

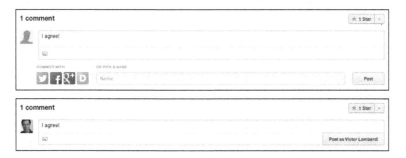

FIGURE 3.10a,b
An example of leaving a comment using Sign In with Twitter (a). If I'm already signed in to Twitter, clicking the Twitter icon here simply updates this page to show that I'm signed in (b). There is nothing to type, no pop-up window, and no extra permissions to grant.

Even better, people can transfer data between other services and Facebook or Twitter once these connections are established. For example, someone could synchronize their relationship status on Facebook with their profile on a dating site, or take a photo with an app on their mobile phone and have it appear in their Facebook stream. And the tight control Facebook and Twitter exert over the design means it looks and acts the same every time it's used.

These technologies offer vastly superior experiences. However, Charlie Cheever, manager of the Facebook Connect team, admitted one problem they found during testing: "*Connect with Facebook* leaves most users with one question. 'What does "connect" mean?'"[12] But that question hasn't kept people from using it. By December 2010, Facebook Connect had been implemented on 2 million websites serving 250 million people, and was growing at a rate of 10,000 new websites a day (Figure 3.11).[13]

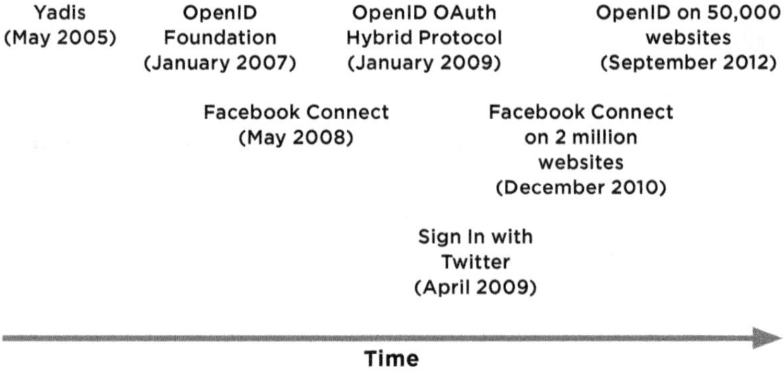

Yadis (May 2005)	OpenID Foundation (January 2007)	OpenID OAuth Hybrid Protocol (January 2009)	OpenID on 50,000 websites (September 2012)

Facebook Connect
(May 2008)

Facebook Connect
on 2 million
websites
(December 2010)

Sign In with
Twitter
(April 2009)

Time

FIGURE 3.11
OpenID and competitors over time.

Evolution

The OpenID Foundation managed the technology standard and was successful in popularizing it. But although they cited usability as a goal, it was only one of many goals and didn't receive enough attention compared with efforts to make the technology platform-agnostic and to make OpenID available on more websites.[14]

That changed in 2009. A new OpenID design was introduced, one that functioned more like Facebook Connect. Combined with OAuth, another new technology, the OpenID OAuth Hybrid Protocol combined OpenID's ability to sign in with OAuth's ability to exchange information between websites and other services. The design hid the URI field and allowed two-click sign-in (Figure 3.12). Like Facebook Connect, the new OpenID used a pop-up window to request permission rather than redirect people to another page. MySpace testing verified this was a better way, reporting that "most users felt more comfortable with the pop-up version of this screen vs. the Redirect version (even when they didn't notice the difference between a pop-up and a redirect)."[15]

Plaxo, the online address book service, tested the new OpenID with customers signing in to their service. The result was a 92 percent success rate, which was so good that Plaxo's marketing department insisted the test design stay live.

This second version of OpenID was a massive improvement in usability. But it was far less commonly used compared with the Facebook and Twitter methods.

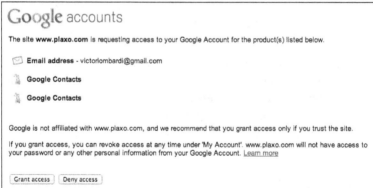

FIGURE 3.12a,b
Signing in at Plaxo.com using the revised two-click version of OpenID (a). Clicking the Google button brings up a pop-up window (b). Clicking the "Grant access" button closes this pop-up window and the visitor is signed in to Plaxo.

Lessons

An Unethical Use of Technology

The OpenID Foundation must get credit both for having good intentions and for solving several tricky technical problems. But by ignoring the experience of people using OpenID and then fixing it too late, those in charge of the technology doomed it to failure.

It's easy to find reports of frustration with the initial OpenID design online.[16] With 50,000 sites using the technology and a billion OpenID accounts, one can imagine the amount of pain and lost productivity. To get a sense of the scale, let's assume only a fifth of those 1 billion accounts represent individuals who actively tried OpenID and had difficulty getting it to work. And let's assume they had difficulty only on one site and on one occasion. Let's also assume that each of those occasions lasted only two minutes.

That's 761 years of frustrating experience.[17]

The actual number might be more or less, but any reasonable estimate is shockingly large. Depressingly large. I would even say unethically large. Although it's possible that OpenID was a good experience for some people, others paid a high price to test this technology. That's fine for early adopters who choose to try unproven technology, but OpenID was harmful to the general public on the Internet. There is no reason that tests like the ones Yahoo! conducted could not have been performed by the OpenID Foundation years earlier. Testing with a small number of people early on is less damaging than experimenting on millions of people with an untried product.

Every new medium experiences some experimentation, and the Internet is certainly a giant example of many simultaneous experiments. But part of experimentation is testing, and it's irresponsible engineering to release an untested design to the general public. We design products to be used by people. If we intend for people to use the thing we build, we need to make sure they can.

How It Failed

We know *why* OpenID failed—using it was a miserable experience. How that experience came about is worth learning from.

OpenID *was not* a failure in its original context of serving LiveJournal bloggers. They all had a URI of their blog that they identified with, and they could use that URI to sign in and comment across the entire sphere of LiveJournal blogs. And it's probably safe to assume that bloggers in 2005 were at least a little more technically proficient than average. The first point of failure was thinking that OpenID could be easily adopted by a general population of nonbloggers using disparate sites across the Web.

Almost all the other reasons for failure were organizational. As a nonprofit, the OpenID Foundation didn't have the resources that Facebook or Twitter brought to the challenge. If they did, they might have had enough people and money to solve the design problems at the beginning.

But even if OpenID had access to the same resources, it may not have mattered. Chris Messina, an OpenID Foundation board member, pointed out that "for OpenID to succeed, it must be developed with the involvement of many different groups, each with slightly different ideas, objectives, and release cycles. Unlike Facebook Connect, OpenID is essentially *consensus technology*. To advance, it must secure and maintain the buy-in *and* adoption of many parties on every forward step."[18] That decision-making style just isn't conducive to good design.

Decentralization was a fundamental tenet of how OpenID performed authentication, but that same principle of decentralization was extended to the interface design, giving providers and sites that used OpenID too much latitude in the design of key registration and sign-in pages. Contrast that with Facebook, which requires developers to follow the Facebook Connect specification.

Additionally, the OpenID Foundation became distracted with a large government project,[19] and subsequently the culture of the organization shifted. Messina later reflected:

> The thing that I regret the most about my last two years on the board is how internalized and secretive the workings of the OpenID Foundation have become. . . . It's become more corporate. And the result was more backdoor politicking and much less consultation or coordination with the community. . . .
>
> This has to do with our shift towards—as Executive Director Don Thibeau puts it—"The Mother of All Use Cases"—that is, the use of OpenID by the United States federal government. By switching our focus from more immediate consumer-facing applications of OpenID, we dropped the thread on use cases that offer the most universal appeal to smaller businesses and individuals—the very folks who had begun to invest in and benefit from the convenience that OpenID promised.[20]

Getting It Right Next Time

Widespread technology standards cannot sidestep experience research and testing. Technology standards organizations like the OpenID Foundation need to incorporate product testing before they release a specification when the standard will directly impact people's experience.

Testing is relatively easy and fast these days. As the Web grew, so did the availability of people with the skills to perform usability testing. Simple tests like those done at Yahoo! and MySpace can be planned, performed, and reported on in about two weeks. We now have technologies that allow remote testing so researchers and participants can be in two different geographic locations. And the emergence of lean and agile methods have made it easier to test, refine the prototype, and test again to iteratively find a better experience. Technical organizations could conduct tests by partnering with design organizations, such as the User Experience Professionals Association, the Interaction Design Association, or the Information Architecture Institute.

I don't mean to imply the fix is an easy one. As a designer and product manager, I know that crafting a technology standard that addresses a myriad of technical, functional, and organizational constraints with an effective interface design is difficult work, and OpenID eventually cleared that hurdle. But ethics compels us to ask ourselves some tough questions: *By spreading this technology are we doing more harm than good? Would the world be a better place if we didn't release this?*

As 37Signals wrote when they discontinued their use of OpenID, "We're sad to see OpenID go. The promise was grand. Life would be simpler if we only had one login, but in this case, the cure was worse than the disease."[21]

Summary

What it was: The first version of OpenID was a decentralized, open standard for using one set of credentials for signing in to websites and other services. The goal was to replace the need to remember a username and password for each service people registered with online. Approximately 50,000 sites integrated OpenID and more than 1 billion OpenID accounts were created.[22] Volunteers created the technology standard, and several companies worked to implement it.

Why the experience failed: The first version was too difficult to use in several ways. The process for registering and signing in was non-standard and sometimes confusing. It required people to remember a URI such as http://myOpenIDprovider.com/VictorLombardi as well as the name of the OpenID service that provided the URI. So although the concept sought a great increase in usability, each instance of the OpenID experience was too difficult to realize the overall benefit of using it all the time.

The underlying cause: The technology was transferred from a niche application where it made sense to a general audience without testing it first. The standards organization lost their focus on the original goal. They prioritized solving technical issues and marketing over usability, and so waited too long before providing a usable version.

The lesson: A robust security standard with effective marketing but wrapped in poor usability is a recipe for disaster that causes widespread suffering. Any technology standard that will impact people's experience needs to undergo product testing before release to the public. In the end, poor usability can erase years of thorough technical work.

CHAPTER 4

Platform
Follows People

> Solve a real problem and the world is yours.
>
> —Aaron Patzer, founder of Mint.com

Wouldn't you love to launch a product and almost immediately become the leader in your market? That's what happened to Wesabe in November 2006 when the company released its online personal financial management Web application. Wesabe accumulated a long list of compelling advantages, such as a devoted community of people who passionately helped one another save money, the ability to import and analyze bank data, and an iPhone app. The company raised $4.7 million in venture capital[1] and, unlike many start-ups, generated some revenue.[2] But by July 2010 the service closed. What happened? This is a story of intense competition, contrasting design solutions, and how a Web 2.0 approach to building a business was beaten by an old-fashioned Web 1.0 approach.

Wesabe

Wesabe.com was an online service that helped people gather all their financial information in one place to better understand it and make better financial decisions (Figure 4.1). The website leveraged the wisdom of the crowd by pooling tips and recommendations from the community on the site.

FIGURE 4.1

Wesabe's Merchant Comparison screen helped people find the best stores for their needs.

In a world of personal finance dominated by Quicken, which is installed on a computer and requires manual data entry, Wesabe made it possible to automate tasks and analyze financial information in entirely new ways.

The Design

The essential experience of Wesabe consisted of two main interactions. First, using a program installed on your computer, you could securely download data from your bank onto your computer; the program could then upload data to the Wesabe website (Figure 4.2). As a new company in a security-sensitive industry, this method assured people that their passwords and their data were safe.

FIGURE 4.2
Using the Wesabe Uploader to send data downloaded from a bank to the Wesabe website.

The second interaction took place on the website, where people could connect with the Wesabe community on message boards to ask questions, share tips, and stay abreast of personal financial news. Even better, the website aggregated financial data from all Wesabe accounts, analyzed it, and recommended to its members ways to better manage their money. A simple example is tagging: if Wesabe recognized that many people were tagging Starbucks stores with the term "food," it would suggest to other members that they tag Starbucks transactions as "food" as well. This made it easy to track how much was being spent on food. You can see a video demonstration of Wesabe at http://rfld.me/VZikXP.

Initial reactions to the service were mostly positive among individuals and the media. Jane J. Kim wrote in the *Wall Street Journal* about a 26-year-old environmental engineer from Cincinnati who used Wesabe and received helpful tips from other people on reducing debt and cutting spending: "One of our goals was to pay off all our debt, and we're almost there."[3] A 29-year-old software engineer in Chicago said, "The idea of looking at a ledger and seeing a check number, that's really boring. But being able to say, 'I'm trying to spend less money at Amazon,' and seeing how many people are also trying to save money at Amazon is a better way to quantify the numbers to me."

A Key Usability Failure

Although the company proved its ability to launch modern, innovative features, Wesabe also suffered usability problems. By mid-2007 people were voicing their frustration over having to download their data from their bank and then upload it to Wesabe.

In July 2007 Wesabe launched a Firefox Web browser extension that made this task easier but still not as easy as it could be (Figure 4.3).[4] Here's a typical complaint voicing the frustration around importing bank data:

> If it's going to be huge, the service is going to have to be friendlier and more intuitive to mainstream adults. Download-ing bank statements or using the Wesabe Uploader seems to be clumsy and generally easier said than done. Is automatic updating an impossible security hurdle? That's what would keep me using it.[5]

FIGURE 4.3
The Wesabe Firefox browser extension.

And a product review from NotebookReview.com reported, "This, unfor-tunately, is where the wheels started to come off. Much like AceMoney, Wesabe asks that you manually download a data file from your bank and then manually upload that same file to Wesabe."[6]

At the time, Wesabe founder Marc Hedlund vigorously defended this data import method, explaining that it offered people more control over their data, avoided the reliability problems of using third-party data transfer software, and avoided costs that helped Wesabe keep the service free and ad-free.[7]

But there were also business reasons behind this decision. In a blog post written after Wesabe's closure, Hedlund reflected,

We chose not to work with Yodlee. . . .

Yodlee is a company that provides automatic financial data aggregation as a web service. They screen-scrape bank web sites (that is, read the payee and amount and date by parsing them out of the bank's web site, writing a custom parser for each bank they support). When we talked to Yodlee in 2006, the company was crumbling, having failed to get acquired and losing executives. They were also very aggressive in negotiation, telling us they would give us six months' service nearly free and then tell us the final price we'd be charged going forward. Since they had effectively no competitors, we didn't believe we should tie our company to a single-source provider, especially one in very bad business shape.[8]

Opportunities and Costs

Despite this usability issue, Wesabe was an innovative product, and the summer of 2007 turned into an exciting time for the company. It launched a Facebook app that created an additional route into its group discussions.[9] But strategically the big move for Wesabe was launching a public API, or application programming interface, which let third-party developers access data on its servers and use that data to create new services. These new services would supposedly benefit Wesabe in a number of ways, particularly by attracting new customers. This is now a well-established move in the Web 2.0 playbook—open up your data to other developers who in turn create more services that drive more people to use your service. Flickr, for example, released an open API used in hundreds of applications, helping attract 2 million members to its online photo service. That large customer base helped justify its $40 million acquisition price to Yahoo![10]

When announcing the API, founder Mark Hedlund wrote, "It matters a lot less to us that you use our website than that you use our API."[11] The API could flexibly serve many different audiences, from a company offering complementary services, to an individual who could use Wesabe to transfer bank data into a manageable spreadsheet. But Hedlund's statement reveals a miscalculation by Wesabe—that people would rather do the work to import and massage their data and receive additional functions through the API than step back and leave more personal finance tasks to the system.

At least two companies launched services based on the Wesabe API, but it's not known if they had any positive impact on Wesabe's business.[12]

Web 2.0 Compliant

In June 2007 Wesabe received a combined $4.7 million in venture capital from Union Square Ventures and O'Reilly AlphaTech Ventures, securing their finances for the next two years.[13] The investment from O'Reilly is particularly relevant because Wesabe illustrated a striking number of the tenets laid out in Tim O'Reilly's seminal 2005 article, "What Is Web 2.0"[14]:

- *"Services, not packaged software"*: As opposed to the Quicken model of using installed software, Wesabe kept its services online, in the cloud, in order to make changes quickly and reach other devices such as mobile phones.

- *"Leverage customer self-service and algorithmic data management to scale the business"*: Wesabe used two key methods for serving a large variety of customers: message boards allowed customers to find information themselves and share tips with each other, and the Wesabe engine processed each customer's data to find tips other customers could use. To quote Tim O'Reilly, "The service automatically gets better the more people use it."

- *"Control over unique, hard-to-recreate data sources"*: Once Wesabe aggregated all their data and analyzed it, the company owned a data set full of intelligence they could use to build additional features and products.

- *"Trusting customers as co-developers"*: Wesabe's API let other companies tap the Wesabe system to build additional services, all for free, in order to help people accomplish more.

Although the Web 2.0 approach brought exciting, strategic opportunities, it also spread thin Wesabe's limited resources. For any startup with venture capital, the clock is ticking to accomplish its goal before the money runs out, so Wesabe had to generate enough revenue to sustain the business or improve it enough to attract more venture capital, or else sell the business. This need became more urgent when a new competitor launched, and what began as a race to build a robust Web 2.0 platform turned into a race to provide the best user experience and gain the lion's share of customers.

A New Competitor

Wesabe's 2007 Summer of Love came to an abrupt end with the launch of competitor Mint.com. Even before Mint's launch it was rumored to be the heavyweight in the market. Mint presented its product to the public in September 2007 at TechCrunch40, a technology conference where 40 promising new startup companies unveil and compete for the best new product prize of $50,000. Mint won, and the resulting media attention immediately propelled their website traffic past all competitors (Figure 4.4).

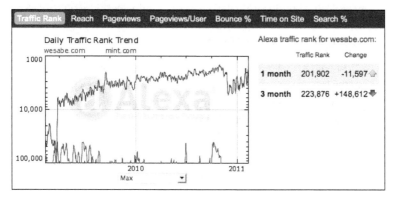

FIGURE 4.4
Traffic rank for Wesabe.com (in blue) versus Mint.com (in red), 2009 and 2010.

In contrast to Wesabe's Web 2.0 approach of publicly launching a beta product and iterating quickly, Mint worked in secrecy, including a *private* beta period, to perfect their product. Mint spent seven months creating a prototype to show investors and raise seed funding, and then worked for another *year* refining the user interface, developing a secure system, and finding an elegant way to connect to thousands of financial institutions. Only then did they launch.

Even while in startup mode, Mint invested in hiring a vice president of product, Aaron Forth, who quickly started redesigning the user interface. He focused first on the flow for setting up new financial institution connections, because that's the initial customer experience and is key for a startup hoping to acquire a lot of new customers (Figure 4.5a).

In contrast to Wesabe's Web 2.0 approach, Mint's path was strikingly conventional. There were three key decisions that improved people's experience:

1. Mint chose to use Yodlee to make importing bank data easy. Mint was probably also aware of the problems Yodlee had as a company but partnered with them anyway, making a bet-the-company decision in favor of a great experience.

2. Mint invested in high-quality visual design (Figure 4.5b) and information architecture. We know from studies on Web credibility that people most often cite visual design and information structure as contributing to credibility, a vital characteristic of a new service entrusted with personal financial data.[15]

3. Mint paid a high price for the mint.com domain name, wanting a name that was a common English-language word, had a positive financial meaning (the place where money is made), and had a positive general meaning (the pleasant-tasting herb). "Mint" is also short and easy to spell. The name "Wesabe" doesn't have these advantages.

FIGURE 4.5a,b
Mint.com can connect to banks and automatically download financial data (a). The Mint.com Trends page charts the automatically aggregated and categorized financial data (b).

A Three-Year Battle

Between 2007 and 2010 other competitors entered the market, but Wesabe and Mint were the leaders. Both companies spent these years pursuing their respective strategies.

Wesabe continued to pursue a broad platform and release cool product extensions at the expense of addressing their core usability and design shortcomings. It launched a desktop widget that streamed real-time account balance and transaction updates, but the widget only worked for the minority of people who used Macs. It also let users update their data via a message on Twitter—for example, "@Wesabe $12 Starbucks (lunch expense)" (Figure 4.6). Although Twitter later exploded in popularity, at the time there were only two million accounts, a small percentage of which would also use Wesabe, use this feature, and remember the syntax for typing the message.

FIGURE 4.6
Updating Wesabe budgeting data with a message on Twitter.

Wesabe launched an iPhone app that received favorable reviews (Figure 4.7). But as with the Twitter integration, this was an additional channel that reinforced their key usability problem of having to manually enter data into the system.

In March 2009 Wesabe launched Springboard, a white-label version of its service "designed specifically for banks and credit unions that want to add personal finance management (PFM) tools to their online banking sites."[16] Reverse-engineering this decision, we can guess Wesabe calculated the day its venture capital would run out and launched Springboard in an attempt to generate revenue and sustain the business. Unfortunately just a month before, competitor Geezeo launched its own white-label service. Geezeo, however, decided to pivot its business entirely in this new direction and focus on business-to-business rather than business-to-consumer services while Wesabe tried to stretch to serve both audiences.

In December 2008 Mint also released an iPhone app, the design of which was so good Apple installed it on the iPhones in the Apple Store (Figure 4.8).[17] Other than this, Mint's priorities were remarkably different from Wesabe's. Mint focused on the core product—for example, launching a feature to track investments. It also pursued marketing deals such as co-branding with Motley Fool and arranging a link on Yahoo!'s homepage, resulting in the company's largest number of new registrations in a single day. The continued increase in customers enabled Mint to raise more money: $12 million in 2008 and another $14 million in 2009, which helped it to comfortably run the business in the face of an economic recession.

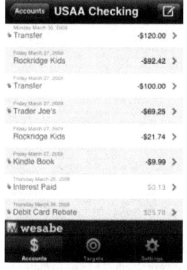

FIGURE 4.7

The Wesabe iPhone app.

FIGURE 4.8

The Mint.com iPhone app.

In short, Mint focused on strengthening the core features that served its target audience and marketing that strength. After two years, it paid off. On September 14, 2009, Intuit acquired Mint for $170 million. After the acquisition, Mint continued to expand and serve customers.

By November 2009 Wesabe had exhausted its invested funds and continued to run the business on a modest revenue stream. But by mid-2010, Wesabe had failed to generate enough income to operate reliably and the service was closed in July (Figure 4.9). As Mark Hedlund wrote at the time,

In recent months Wesabe has been operating on a shoestring budget. . . . While the site has remained online and we continue to hear from people who find it helpful, we have not been able to provide the support people need to use it for something so central as financial management. I've felt especially terrible that some members have a good initial experience but then hit a problem, often after investing many hours, and aren't able to get help with it. That's obviously a bad experience, and not what we want to offer.[18]

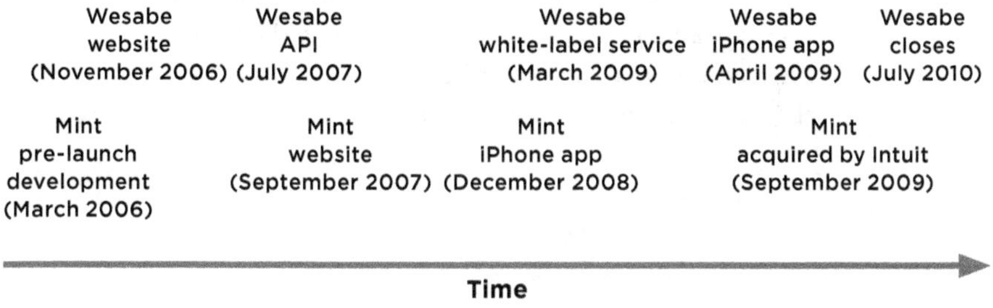

Wesabe website (November 2006)	Wesabe API (July 2007)		Wesabe white-label service (March 2009)	Wesabe iPhone app (April 2009)	Wesabe closes (July 2010)
Mint pre-launch development (March 2006)	Mint website (September 2007)	Mint iPhone app (December 2008)		Mint acquired by Intuit (September 2009)	

⟶

Time

FIGURE 4.9

Wesabe.com and Mint.com timeline.

Lessons

Did Wesabe fail? It built a very good product that people found valuable for almost four years. So in one sense Wesabe was a success. It is probably more accurate to say Mint beat Wesabe with a superior customer experience. When Mint launched with a better design and seamless bank data importing, suddenly the bar was raised for personal financial tools, and what Wesabe offered customers wasn't enough by comparison. An additional misfortune for customers was losing the Wesabe service entirely when it was closed down.

Solving the Best Problem

Mint and Wesabe addressed the same high-level goal: to improve personal financial management. But within that problem were different subproblems—Wesabe wanted to help people edit and organize their data, but this solution still resulted in a lot of work for customers. Mint accepted the burden of organizing the data so people could focus on understanding their financial situation. People preferred the solution Mint offered.

Compete on Experience

In any competitive market people will naturally compare their experience with other similar products. As service providers, the question to ask is not "Are people using this product having a good experience?" but instead, "Are people using this product having the best experience of any product in the market?" And we need to ask this question whenever a new competitor comes on the scene. Wesabe was focused on beating Quicken, but then Mint launched and Wesabe never caught up.

Mint applied this lesson by learning from Wesabe for 10 months before launching. Although a first-mover can sometimes grab a critical mass of market share and, particularly in the financial industry, lock in customers who have invested time entering data, in this case the first-mover Wesabe may actually have been at a disadvantage. As Hedlund wrote,

> There's a lot to be said for not rushing to market, and learning from the mistakes the first entrants make. Shipping a "minimum viable product" immediately and learning from the market directly makes good sense to me, but engaging with and supporting customers is anything but free. Observation can be cheaper. Mint (and some others) did well by seeing where we screwed up, and waiting to launch until they had a better approach.[19]

Platform Follows People

Wesabe created a beautiful long-term strategy that applied Web 2.0 principles in the hope of helping people and revolutionizing a market. But this long-term plan led the company to build an elaborate infrastructure with an API for developers and a white-label version for banks, all with the limited resources of a startup. This strategy hindered Wesabe's ability to provide its most important customers—individual consumers—a great experience.

In a new, competitive market like online personal financial management there's a race to acquire a critical mass of customers before your competition. Once this is accomplished, a company has the luxury of expanding in new directions. Mint, by emphasizing strong tactics in the short term, reached critical mass first. Hedlund summed this up:

> Between the worse data aggregation method and the much higher amount of work Wesabe made you do, it was far easier to have a good experience on Mint, and that good experience came far more quickly. Everything I've mentioned—not being dependent on a single source provider, preserving users'

privacy, helping users actually make positive change in their financial lives—all of those things are great, rational reasons to pursue what we pursued. But none of them matter if the product is harder to use, since most people simply won't care enough or get enough benefit from long-term features if a shorter-term alternative is available.[20]

The great Internet platforms of our time—Google, Facebook, and Twitter—didn't start as platforms, but rather as small services. They attracted a large following on the strength of that simpler initial experience. Only once they gained that following could they leverage it into a platform.

For example, Google's platform allows it to sell and serve contextual advertisements alongside search results. It can display posts, photos, profiles, and conversations from Google+ within search results. And it can display maps and other useful information. But all that is possible only because the original search function attracted a giant audience of people who appreciated a simple, easy, fast experience. Once Google had a large audience, it could expand from search into an entire platform of related products. Strategically speaking, platform follows people.

What Really Matters

In the end, Mark Hedlund is a generous entrepreneur who leaves us with pragmatic advice:

> I am, of course, enormously sad that Wesabe lost and the company closed. I don't agree with those who say you should learn from your successes and mostly ignore your failures; nor do I agree with those who obsess over failures for years after (as I have done in the past). I'm hoping that by writing this all out I can offload it from my head and hopefully help inform other people who try to start companies in the future.
>
> You'll hear a lot about why company A won and company B lost in any market, and in my experience, a lot of the theories thrown about—even or especially by the participants—are utter crap. A domain name doesn't win you a market; launching second or fifth or tenth doesn't lose you a market. You can't blame your competitors or your board or the lack of or excess of investment. Focus on what really matters: making customers happy with your product as quickly as you can, and helping them as much as you can after that. If you do those better than anyone else out there you'll win.[21]

Summary

What it was: Wesabe.com was an online service that helped people gather all their financial information in one place to better understand it and make better financial decisions. Wesabe leveraged several Web 2.0 techniques, such as creating a self-service community on the website. About 100,000 people used the service, and $4.7 million was invested. It launched in November 2006 and closed in July 2010.

Why the experience failed: Wesabe solved the problem of aggregating financial data and helping people learn from it, but competitor Mint.com solved the same basic problem a different way that was much easier for customers to use.

The underlying cause: Wesabe created a platform based on Web 2.0 principles of openness, participation, and rich data, and leveraged that platform to extend their business in several directions. Mint focused on creating a beautiful, easy-to-use service that attracted many more customers.

The lessons: For any customer problem we address, there are multiple ways to solve it, and we need to spend time at the conceptual design stage of problem solving to find the preferred solution.

Platforms without people are worthless. Platforms must start as simpler, effective functions that build an audience. Only then can they be extended with related services. Platform follows people.

In an ongoing business that competes by providing a positive experience, a company needs to regularly benchmark the experience of their customers versus the competition to ensure it's the best.

Design for Reflection

Nothing succeeds like success. [Rien ne réussit comme le succès.]

—French proverb

When Sony introduced the Walkman portable stereo in 1979, it was a sensation. We didn't expect that a device small enough to clip to our belts could play cassettes in stereo and sound almost as good as our home systems. It went on to become a commercial success for years.

The Walkman experience went beyond how the device looked, felt, and sounded. Using it gave us more control over our environment, control over who we chose to speak with or even to make eye contact with in public. It allowed us to bring mood-altering music with us as we moved about in the world, changing how we acted and how we felt about our activities. This phenomenon has been called the *Walkman effect*.[1]

Could a similar device have the same experiential impact in the 21st century? If so, what would it be like? And how would others hope or try to compete with it?

Microsoft Zune Media Player

Let's say it's 2006 and you're in the market for a portable media player to listen to music. Several models are being offered by Apple, Toshiba, SanDisk, Microsoft, and others. You don't own a lot of music now but you do enjoy a wide variety, so Microsoft's Zune Music Pass service is attractive because it offers unlimited listening to millions of songs, all for a low monthly fee. The Zune player is compatible with your Windows computer, has features comparable to other devices, and is competitively priced at $250 for the 30 gigabyte (GB) version. So you opt for a Zune in the unique brown color.

This is the perfectly logical story that Microsoft would have liked to have seen repeated many times, hundreds of millions of times, like the original Sony Walkman in its day. But that's not what happened.

The Design

Microsoft launched its Zune portable media player in 2006. Because it is more of a software than a hardware company, Microsoft partnered with Toshiba to modify the Toshiba Gigabeat S (Figure 5.1). The Gigabeat played music and video files and FM radio, displayed photos, and had excellent audio circuits. The software was easy to use. The hardware came with state-of-the-art 30GB or 60GB memory capacity, was attractive, and was both smaller and lighter than the market leader, the Apple iPod. It also ran the Windows Mobile operating system and had strong compatibility with Microsoft's Windows XP for syncing the Gigabeat with a PC, making this partnership a logical choice. The Gigabeat was generally well regarded and was an Editor's Choice at the consumer technology website CNET.com.

The Microsoft Zune was a better Gigabeat. The Zune hardware featured a unique industrial design with a rubberized plastic case that was highly scratch-resistant. It was painted a different color on the inside and the outside, resulting in a subtle two-tone look. The screen, measured diagonally at three inches, was bigger than the iPod's (Figure 5.2).

The Zune added interesting features such as the ability to wirelessly send songs and pictures to another Zune to share them with friends.

FIGURE 5.1
The Toshiba Gigabeat S, the basis of the first Zune.

FIGURE 5.2
The original Zune in brown.

Perhaps the biggest addition was Zune's ability to access media purchased in Microsoft's online media store, the Marketplace. There you could buy a song for $1, or with the Zune Music Pass for $15 per month you could download as many songs as would fit on your Zune. And the songs would also play on your Windows PC or Xbox.

The Experience

The experience of using a Zune was also very good. The software was easy to use and attractive, using the full screen to display an album cover when playing a song.

The unique case was pleasing to the touch. The brown model with a green tinge became the iconic Zune, a color combination some mocked but others loved.

The audio sounded great and the screen looked good. You can watch a video of a customer's first experience using a Zune at http://rfld.me/X90pPD.

Of course there were hiccups as with any new product. Initially the PC software didn't support podcasts. And although the device had Wi-Fi, you could only use it to send files Zune-to-Zune and not to connect to a network to play songs from the Marketplace. Until more people owned Zunes, there was no one to share with.

However, these issues were comparable to faults in other devices, including the iPod, and they were later addressed. In 2011 I researched owners' experiences with their Zunes. No serious criticisms came to the fore when owners discussed their experiences. I heard faint praise for the device and its companion service: "It's a nice-looking device"; "The audio quality is very good"; "I can subscribe to their music service."

Likewise, sentiment expressed online in social media was mostly positive: 68 percent love versus 32 percent hate.[2]

Reactions

Journalists' opinions of the first Zune were strikingly consistent: the Zune was good but not great.

Walter Mossberg in the *Wall Street Journal* found some bugs and missing features, but liked the "very good user interface.... It has only a few buttons and is quite intuitive to use.... [T]he entire interface is more colorful and visually satisfying [than the iPod]."[3]

David Pogue of the *New York Times* found similar faults and similar highlights,[4] as did Nate Anderson at *Ars Technica*, who wrote, "If you're looking for an attractive music player with a great screen and a fine interface, the Zune is worth a look."[5]

The Competition

Starting in 1997, an assortment of companies began mass-producing portable media players. Apple introduced its iPod in 2001 and was itself considered late to the party, but the iPod quickly became the market leader (Figure 5.3). The iPod was set apart mostly through a simplified industrial design that featured a click wheel instead of buttons to scroll through song lists. Rather than complicate the device with functions to manage your music library, all music management was done in the iTunes desktop software.

By 2006 when the Zune came out, the iPod was already on version "5.5." Like the Zune, it was also priced at $250 for a 30GB version. They even shared the same Wolfson audio chip, so the audio fidelity was the same.

FIGURE 5.3
The Apple iPod, a 30GB version circa 2006.

Compared to the Zune, the iPod had a smaller screen that wasn't as bright, though it was sharper with better contrast. The iPod did not have an FM tuner. And Apple's equivalent of the Marketplace, the iTunes Store, offered no way to subscribe to unlimited music.

On the other hand, the iPod had more apps, from an address book and a calendar to a variety of games. The iTunes Store boasted a larger music library with movies and TV shows. The iPod worked with both Macs and Windows (Apple added Windows support for the iPod in 2003; Microsoft added Mac support for the Zune in 2011).

On paper the Zune and the iPod were evenly matched, though in the reviews of many journalists the iPod had the edge with fewer bugs and a larger media library.

Evolution

Over the course of 2007 and 2008, Microsoft released two more generations of the Zune. They were custom designed and manufactured by an original equipment manufacturer, Flextronics, instead of being modified from an existing player. The new Zunes used flash memory instead of hard drives so they were smaller and more reliable. A touch-sensitive scroll wheel like the iPod's replaced the original front-mounted buttons. Most important, the Wi-Fi was updated so it could access Wi-Fi networks. The new devices also took advantage of their FM radios by letting people tag the songs they liked and then purchase them wirelessly from the Marketplace, something the iPod couldn't do.

David Pogue summed up most journalists' reactions: "[T]he Zune has become almost a cross between music player and satellite radio. Wireless streaming, capturing from the radio, channel subscriptions, recommendations—if you're a heavy music consumer and you're willing to pay $15 a month forever, it's just the best."[6] But otherwise, "The Zune store still lacks movies, downloadable programs, gift certificates, monthly allowances or any way to rate podcasts to guide fellow visitors. And the player still has no stopwatch, alarm clock, volume limiter, calendar, address book, note pad or external-hard-drive mode. . . . The iPod still wins."

In September 2009 Microsoft released the Zune HD, a completely redesigned version that could play HD video and HD radio (Figure 5.4). Like the current generation of smartphones, it employed a touchscreen interface and beautiful new software on the device—including built-in apps—and for the desktop.

FIGURE 5.4
The Zune HD.

Journalists agreed the Zune HD had caught up to the iPod:

> [T]he Zune HD player isn't perfect, but it's every bit as joyful, polished and satisfying as its rival.
>
> —David Pogue, *New York Times*[7]

> The Zune HD is a great-looking little player, and users will especially appreciate its Quickplay menu [for one-click access to volume, track forward/back and play/pause controls], rich collection of artist information, and mesmerizing screen.
>
> —Katherine Boehret, *Wall Street Journal*[8]

> The Zune HD delivers one of the best portable music and video experiences money can buy.
>
> —Donald Bell, CNET[9]

Meanwhile, each iteration of the iPod featured more advanced hardware and software, first with a more elegant click wheel, then a touchscreen, and then a camera that could be used for photos, video, and video conferencing. The iPod had gone beyond music and video and now ran iPhone apps, 75,000 of which were available in the App Store. The pace of Zune app releases was much slower: by August 2011 the Zune Marketplace had 63 apps for Zune HD, of which 41 were games.

Quantitative Results

The sales data dramatically demonstrates consumer preference for the iPod over the Zune (Figure 5.5).

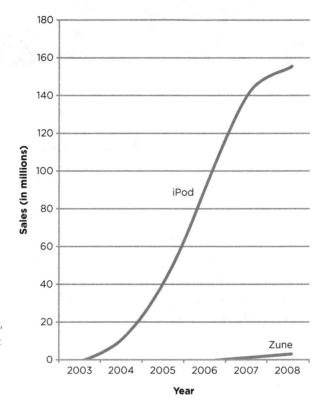

FIGURE 5.5
Cumulative sales for the iPod and the Zune, 2003–2008. Microsoft didn't release specific sales numbers for the Zune beyond 2008.

There's no public information to tell us exactly how much Microsoft spent developing the Zune or how much the company made selling it (Microsoft declined to comment on this case study). In its financial reports the Zune falls into the Entertainment and Devices Division from which we can tease out a picture of what happened financially.

For the fiscal year ending June 2007 Microsoft reported, "Zune (which was launched in November 2006), consumer hardware and software, and TV platforms revenue increased $539 million or 65%."[10] Although revenue went up, the division overall lost money partially due to "Zune launch-related expenses" and "headcount-related costs." Losses early on are typical for any new product because of significant new product development and marketing costs.

The following year, 2008, the division increased revenue and made a profit, but that increase is attributed primarily to higher sales of the Xbox 360 game platform.[11]

Starting in fiscal year 2009, Microsoft's "non-gaming" revenue, which includes the Zune, fell hundreds of millions each year: $292 million in 2009, $300 million in 2010, and $197 million in 2011.[12]

Microsoft announced in October 2011 they would discontinue the Zune device, stating that, "going forward, Windows Phone will be the focus of our mobile music and video strategy, and that we will no longer be producing Zune players."[13] Windows Phone was a new smartphone platform that used the Zune's software interface design.

At the time, some journalists were predicting that the era of the personal media player was nearing its end. Sales of all manufacturers' portable media players were declining, including Apple's. Meanwhile, sales of smartphones were rising sharply. Analysts explained this by pointing out that personal media players had evolved to become smartphones without the phone. People were now using their smartphones to play media. To some extent that's true. Still, Apple sold more than 15.4 million iPods in the fourth quarter of 2011 when the Zune was discontinued, more than the total number of Zunes sold.[14] Apple continued to sell four different iPod models and released new versions through 2012.

Lessons

How could such a competent product, especially in the later Zune HD incarnation, not gain more than 10 percent market share? If the Zune was designed well and the experience of using it was good, then why didn't people buy more of them to get the Zune experience? To understand this, we need to look more deeply into what makes up a customer's experience.

Reflective Design

Don Norman, in his book *Emotional Design*, divides the experience of a product into three levels of cognition: visceral, behavioral, and reflective. Visceral reactions are the immediate, sometimes instinctual feelings people have to their perceptions. A delicious food, an attractive person, and the aroma of flowers all cause visceral reactions. The Zune—the color and texture of the case, the video on the screen, the quality of sound—satisfied on a visceral level.

Behavioral experience is how people feel when using something. When a product performs well, people have a good behavioral experience. Norman outlines four components of good behavioral design:

1. Function: How well does the product perform the function for which it is designed?

2. Understandability: How well do people understand what the product is and what it does?

3. Usability: How easily can people use the product?

4. Physical feel: Does the way the product feels help people use it?

Although the initial Zune had some faults, later versions were behaviorally quite nice. The one major "function" drawback in the early Zune years was the smaller amount of media available in the Marketplace compared to the iTunes Store. But even if the Marketplace was of equal size, I don't believe it would have made the Zune a success because of people's reflective experience of the Zune.

Reflective experience, as Norman describes it, "covers a lot of territory":

> It is all about message, about culture, and about the meaning of a product or its use. For one, it is about the meaning of things, their personal remembrances something evokes. For another, very different thing, it is about self-image and the message a product sends to others.[15]

The Zune failed on the reflective level.

In my 2011 research with Zune owners, no one talked about how it made them feel good or think differently about listening to their music, which were common responses when the iPod was released. They didn't proudly show me the device, and in fact they were a little sheepish about not buying the iPod. The Zune simply performed a function for them.

Technology writer Robert Scoble noted the social aspects of the device, rating it on "Conversationality: (Does it cause a conversation). Here Apple wins with the white headphones hands down."[16] He went on to look at another typical social experience:

> My son is a good gauge of whether Zune has a chance. Peer pressure is hyper strong to have an iPod. If you show up to school with something that isn't an iPod you aren't cool. Now, that'll change if kids think there's something cool or better. So far nothing I showed Patrick about Zune got him interested.

Technology writer Anil Dash zeroed in on one design detail to compliment the Zune's visceral design while lodging a general criticism of the Zune's reflective design:

> Microsoft has done a good job of achieving many of these goals, while still making an overall experience that's strangely unsatisfying. To me, this is epitomized by one fact: *There's a brown Zune.*
>
> In person, the device has a rich, warm color. The green tinge is innovative; I've never seen a consumer electronics device that tries for such a complicated, organic palette, and it's pulled off wonderfully. But instead of calling the color chocolate, or something else compelling and attractive, they named it *brown*, a color that has few positive associations except (possibly) UPS. Chocolate is desirable, and fuels passions. It's even a little bit sinful.[17]

Becoming Reflective

The iPod pounced on the market with reflective design early enough to establish a monopoly. In 2009 David Pogue wrote, "The question is whether Microsoft will stick it out long enough to close the catalog gap, the ecosystem gap, and the image gap."[18] He goes on to answer that question:

> If this thing came out in a parallel universe where the iPod didn't exist, it would be hailed as a god.
>
> . . . The problem is the iPod's head start—its catalog of music, movies, apps and accessories are ridiculously superior to the Zune's—and the Zune's reputation as the player for weirdos and losers. Among the under-25 set, "Zune" is a punch line.

The iPod didn't achieve that reflective status by accident. Apple's advertising influenced how we felt about the device. These messages were less about the device (e.g., "30GB") and more about the experience ("10,000 songs in your pocket"). The famous "silhouette" ad campaign was a simple, bold visual representation of our experience of the iPod and barely mentioned the device (Figure 5.6).

FIGURE 5.6
Apple's "silhouette" ad campaign for the iPod began in 2003. The television ads featured dancing silhouettes holding white iPods and wearing white earphones. The ads de-emphasized the design of the device and focused on the experience.

In a market category with the awkward name "personal media players" and products from unfamiliar brands such as Archos and SanDisk, the iPod became a household word, synonymous with the entire category. The physical form inspired children's toys (Figure 5.7) and jewelry (Figure 5.8).

The Zune could match the iPod on the visceral and behavioral levels but it never caught up on the reflective level—the personal and cultural meaning, the reflection of the iPod.

FIGURE 5.7
A child's toy fashioned after the iPod includes a scroll wheel and a shuffle function.

FIGURE 5.8
A jewelry designer created earrings by upcycling iPod earphones.

Competing on Reflective Design

What does it take to go head-to-head with an industry leader in consumer electronics on visceral, behavioral, *and* reflective design?

Four billion dollars.

That's how much Microsoft invested to build the Xbox game console business to compete with Sony's PlayStation.[19] There's an interesting contrast between the Zune and the Xbox business outcomes. In 2001 the Xbox went to war with the Sony PlayStation, which, like the iPod, held the lead for several years before Microsoft entered the market. Unlike the Zune, the Xbox hardware and software were developed in-house and included new graphics technology that gave the Xbox a strategic advantage. In 2005 Microsoft released the second Xbox version, the 360, and went to great lengths to achieve world-class industrial design, first by hiring several different firms to submit designs and then hiring two more firms to submit even better ideas (Figure 5.9). The following year Microsoft released the first Zune. Whereas the Xbox found success from all-new designs, the Zune was created by revamping an existing Toshiba media player. The cost to create the Zune business was somewhere in the hundreds of millions of dollars, as compared to the Xbox's $4 billion investment to develop the console and the service, create the marketing campaign, and attract third-party developers to develop games.

And after investing $4 billion, did Microsoft gain the number one position in game console sales? No, the Xbox and the PlayStation competed in a worldwide battle for the number *two* position. The number one spot was grabbed by another new contender, the Nintendo Wii, which outsold both the Xbox and the PlayStation by far.[20] Interestingly, the Wii didn't try to compete with the Xbox and PlayStation in the usual battle of speed or graphics resolution; it featured an innovative wireless motion-sensing controller that was easier to use for less experienced game players. Wii games looked and sounded different (visceral design) and played differently (behavioral design). And as a result, the Wii attracted new audiences, such as adult women, who hadn't been part of the game console demographic (reflective design).[21]

The parallel evolution of products in the game console market provides insight into two strategies for battling an entrenched competitor:

1. Compete directly with a huge capital investment.

2. Compete through a highly differentiated and reflective customer experience.

Microsoft may have intended to pursue the latter strategy for the Zune, but failed to create more than just another iPod competitor.

FIGURE 5.9
The Microsoft Xbox 360.

Summary

What it was: Microsoft launched the Zune portable media player in 2006. The first version was a modified Toshiba Gigabeat S that played music and video files and FM radio, displayed photos, could wirelessly share music and photos with other Zunes, and came in a stylish case. Successive versions were custom designed and manufactured; they added more features while the physical device became smaller and more attractive. The device could connect to the online Zune Marketplace for purchasing music and videos individually or for renting files through a monthly subscription. Microsoft discontinued the device in October 2011 after having invested hundreds of millions of dollars in Zune development.[22] Probably fewer than 15 million Zunes were sold.

Why the experience failed: The Zune looked good and worked well, but the market-leading Apple iPod had a monopoly on our reflective experience. Through beautiful and usable industrial and interaction design, as well as clever advertising, the iPod became a cultural icon that was as much a statement of personal style and identity as it was functional.

The underlying cause: Microsoft tried to differentiate the Zune based on features, such as FM radio and the ability to buy music with a subscription, but the *experience* of the device was never different enough to avoid a direct comparison with the iPod. As a direct competitor, the Zune entered the market too late and with too little investment in the product design, platform, and marketing to challenge the reflective experience of the iPod.

The lesson: Only challenge a strong market leader if you're willing to make a massive investment or develop a highly differentiated product to compete on the basis of reflective experience.

Generate Critical Mass

Years ago at *BYTE* Magazine my friend Ben Smith, who was a Unix greybeard even then (now he's a Unix whitebeard), made a memorable comment that's always stuck with me. We were in the midst of evaluating a batch of LAN email products. "One of these days," Ben said in, I think, 1991, "everyone's going to look up from their little islands of LAN email and see this giant mothership hovering overhead called the Internet."

Increasingly I've begun to feel the same way about the various social networks. How many networks can one person join? How many different identities can one person sanely manage?

—Jon Udell, technology writer, 2007[1]

Until recently the study of how social networks grow was only relevant to academics and large services such as Facebook and Twitter. But now social networks exist for niche categories such as Tony Hawk fans, angel investors, and quilters. Many people benefit from the viability of these social networks, and some create and manage them. So the story of Pownce, Twitter, and the early microblogging services offers valuable lessons.

The dynamics of social networks differ from other markets in a number of ways. One is how they achieve critical mass. If you sell vacuum cleaners or lightbulbs, you need to sell enough units to be profitable. But if you run a social network you need a *critical mass* of the market—a sufficient number of customers interacting with one another to provide value to the network on the whole in a sustainable way. Two people on Facebook is not interesting; a billion people on Facebook is very interesting.

Critical mass as achieved by other products over the last 40 years has been defined as 15 percent of a market, at which point complementary businesses emerge and adoption accelerates and becomes self-sustaining.[2] DVD players, for example, were in 15 percent of households by 2000, enabling businesses such as Netflix to emerge and sell DVD subscription services, further popularizing the DVD format.

Critical mass for social networks is different. In essence, critical mass is achieved when most or all of the people you want to be there are there. Maybe not all your friends and family are on Facebook, but if most are there it becomes a valuable way to share with them. The Path service limits you to 150 friends to encourage you to select high-quality connections. So it's less important that everyone uses Path and more important that people close to you do.

Another way social networks differ from other markets is how they win a slice of the public's attention. Unlike DVD players, it's easy for customers to use more than one social network simultaneously, so one might think that many social networks could coexist. In reality, de facto standards arise. People have limited time and attention and can only participate in so many networks, so they gravitate toward the ones that provide the most value. They may use one or two general networks, such as Facebook and Google+, and a few that focus on specific functions, such as LinkedIn. Within a given topic area, there is only so much room for competing networks. So it's likely that within a given market a social network may need to reach critical mass faster than the competition.

Pownce

Microblogging services are simple services that let people post short messages, usually a maximum of 140 characters, and read messages from others. Microblogs first emerged on the Web around 2006 and grew quickly. The most popular is Twitter, which publicly launched that year.

Pownce launched in June 2007 with a bang, logging about 250,000 visitors in its first month, nearly double the number using Twitter. Such initial popularity is understandable: by this time microblogging was hot and the Pownce founders were popular in the Silicon Valley technology community.

Pownce was partially self-funded and received a small, undisclosed investment from angel investors.[3] Consequently the Pownce team was only a handful of people.

The Design

Though the microblogging function was at the core of the product, Pownce's unique offering was how it combined microblogging with file sharing. Most microblogging services offered only publicly viewable messages, but Pownce allowed you to interact either with everyone or with specific groups of people at a time. You could post a short text message to a group of people instead of to everyone and include an event listing, a link, or a file attachment. And replies to messages were threaded so you could visually follow a conversation as you can in online forums. All of this happened with attractive and functional Web design (Figure 6.1).

Initially Pownce did not have a mobile version and it didn't work via text messaging. But the desktop application let you post and read posts from friends on your computer (Figure 6.2).

FIGURE 6.1

A customer's Pownce home page, July 2007.

FIGURE 6.2

The Pownce desktop client.

Pownce also offered a Pro level of service for $20 per year (Figure 6.3). Pro status allowed you to send files up to 100 megabytes (MB) as opposed to the 10MB limit on the free service. The Pro service was also ad-free, and it let subscribers change the visual theme with different color schemes and background images.

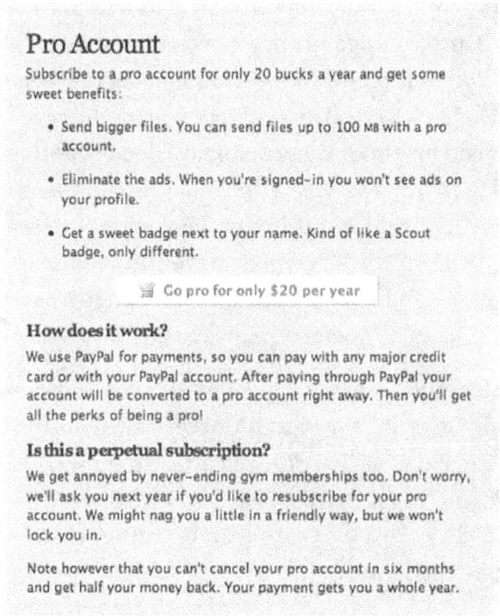

Pro Account

Subscribe to a pro account for only 20 bucks a year and get some sweet benefits:

- Send bigger files. You can send files up to 100 MB with a pro account.

- Eliminate the ads. When you're signed-in you won't see ads on your profile.

- Get a sweet badge next to your name. Kind of like a Scout badge, only different.

> Go pro for only $20 per year

How does it work?

We use PayPal for payments, so you can pay with any major credit card or with your PayPal account. After paying through PayPal your account will be converted to a pro account right away. Then you'll get all the perks of being a pro!

Is this a perpetual subscription?

We get annoyed by never-ending gym memberships too. Don't worry, we'll ask you next year if you'd like to resubscribe for your pro account. We might nag you a little in a friendly way, but we won't lock you in.

Note however that you can't cancel your pro account in six months and get half your money back. Your payment gets you a whole year.

FIGURE 6.3
Pownce's revenue model included selling advertising and Pro Accounts.

The Pownce team demonstrated an impressive development cycle, quickly enhancing existing features, adding themes, and launching a mobile Web version. To avoid overloading its servers and incurring downtime, Pownce gradually released invitations to the service before fully opening up to new customers in January 2008.

In theory, Pownce's microblogging service could have attracted a large general audience while the file-sharing features would have also attracted groups of customers. Once groups adopted and came to rely on its group-oriented features, the thought was that Pownce would enjoy higher customer retention than its competitors.

The Experience

If you've never seen or used Pownce, check out the short video at http://rfld.me/VZiqyG, which demonstrates some of the essential features as seen during one individual's first-time experience.

If you wanted to sign up for Pownce during its first six months, you would have needed an invitation from someone else, such as a friend who was already a member. Once you signed up, you would be able to send out a limited number of invitations of your own. Knowing that services such as Twitter and Facebook were also available, you might have thought, "Where should I spend my time? Where will my friends be? How should I use this differently than other services? To whom should I send invitations?" If you didn't have enough invitations or if not enough of the people you invited signed up, the utility of Pownce was limited compared to e-mail. Pownce had no public timeline to show all updates as Twitter does, so it could be difficult to find new people to connect with.

Many of the features and interactions that are now familiar conventions on the Web were pioneered by sites like Pownce. If you've used Twitter or made status updates on Facebook or Google+, you already know what it was like to use them on Pownce: type in a short message, include a photo, link, or other file, and click "Post it!" Posting and reading others' posts was the majority of the experience.

Once connected to others, you'd receive a deluge of notification e-mails, one for every new friend or new message. But the message text wasn't in the e-mail—you would have to click to the website to read it.

You could also use Pownce in a more peripheral way, such as leaving the desktop application open on your screen to monitor what your friends were saying while you worked or did something else.

Reactions

There was rabid excitement for Pownce before it launched. Twitter connected people in new ways but was simple, and everyone could imagine much more. The demand for Pownce was so high that once the invitation-only period started, existing Pownce members sometimes sold invitations on eBay for $5 or $10 each.

After launch, people made the inevitable comparisons to Twitter:

- Pownce looked better.

- Pownce had more features.

But . . .

- Twitter had more members.

- Twitter had more ways to post and read messages, especially via text messaging.

There's a predictable mix of praise and criticism of Pownce to be found online, from regular use to bug reports.

In a survey of published reviews, about 10 were favorable, 10 were indifferent, and 5 were not favorable.[4] All journalists compared Pownce to Twitter. One of the more prominent publications called it "a well-designed Web and software-based sharing tool" (*PC Magazine*)[5] and another said, "It's extremely well put-together—capable yet easy to get into and use. And useful. And fun. Try it if you can" (CNET).[6]

Michael Arrington's comments on TechCrunch were perhaps the most prescient:

> Services like Twitter and Pownce . . . are highly viral and benefit from the network effect. People want to join the service that all of their friends already use, and so each new user adds value to the network as a whole. By that measure, Twitter is far ahead of Pownce.
>
> Frankly, unless you really like the mobile aspect of Twitter, there isn't a whole lot of difference between the two services. I expect Twitter will add most of the Pownce features in the short term anyway. And many of the unique features of Pownce—like file sharing, group messaging, etc., are handled pretty well already by . . . email. Gmail, for example, lets users send files of up to 20 MB. Pownce lets you send up to 10 MB files, unless you pay for a pro account (then the limit is 100 MB). And email is certainly very useful for private and group messaging.
>
> People use Twitter to quickly tell the world (or at least the people who care) what they are up to and what they are looking at on the web. Like blogging, it's a one-to-many application that works very well. Twitter does that perfectly, and does little else. Pownce does it, too, but all the other features are really just distractions.[7]

The reactions made it clear that Pownce wouldn't succeed or fail based only on its own merits but in a race with the competition.

The Competition

Between 2006 and 2010 several microblogging services were competing for leadership. The most prominent were Jaiku, Google Buzz, Plurk, Identi.ca, and Twitter.

Jaiku was launched in July 2006 and Google acquired the company in October 2007, possibly to acquire the Jaiku staff rather than the product or customers. Google announced in January 2009 that it would not continue Jaiku development and shut it down in January 2012 to focus on Google+.

Google Buzz was launched in February 2010. Like Pownce, you could use Buzz to share publicly or with select friends. The service was criticized widely for privacy concerns and lacked any differentiation or improvement over Facebook or microblogs. Buzz was shut down in December 2011 so the company could focus on Google+.

Plurk launched in May 2008 and features a unique graphical display of status updates that scrolls horizontally. Plurk experienced an initial burst of popularity, but use has since waned. By 2012 two-thirds of its customers were concentrated in Taiwan and India, and traffic remains low.

Identi.ca launched in 2008 and is quite similar to Twitter, but Identi.ca is built on open-source code using open standards. The project is still active, but traffic to the service is low, with 40 percent concentrated in India.

But the most popular of all is Twitter. Compared to Pownce, Twitter is a relatively simple service focused only on microblogging and has a less-refined visual design (Figure 6.4). Unlike Pownce, Twitter offered short message service (SMS) from the beginning, riding the tidal wave of increasing mobile phone and smartphone use.

Kick-starting a social network from scratch is difficult because a small network offers little value. To establish an audience, Twitter targeted early adopters who were eager to test it simply because it was cool new technology. The company found particular success with attendees of the South by Southwest Interactive conference in 2007. Despite not adding significant new features, by 2007 Twitter was steadily growing at a rate of thousands of visitors per month. This even in the face of infamous system downtime, totaling a cumulative six days over the course of 2007 (Figure 6.5).

FIGURE 6.4

A customer's Twitter home page, April 2007.

FIGURE 6.5

When Twitter went down, visitors saw the infamously common
"fail whale."

When Pownce launched in June 2007, the media attention was a tide that raised all boats: traffic at Twitter jumped from about 100,000 to more than 400,000 visitors.

By June 2008 Twitter had received $20 million in funding, enabling the company to build up its team and infrastructure to keep up with customer growth.[8]

Evolution

In July 2007, external developers reverse-engineered the undocumented API (application programming interface) that powered the Pownce desktop application so they could create new services. An API allows third-party developers to integrate data from the host service into another service. Although unexpected, this was great news for Pownce because it meant outside developers would build new services on top of Pownce to attract new members. The next logical step would have been to build an official API to make the job easier for outside developers. But Pownce's reaction to this demand was slow, mainly because of its small staff. Pownce first released a read-only API four months after launch and a full API eight months after launch.

A mobile Web version of Pownce was initially created by an external developer. The small Pownce team gladly accepted the work and launched it in December 2007.[9] At the time, some in the media had already noticed the low traffic to the site and questioned whether the service could continue (Figure 6.6).[10]

Early in 2008 the Pownce team worked to develop a music-sharing service called Pownce.FM (Figure 6.7).[11] It would allow Pownce members to upload songs and then freely browse, play, and download the collection of songs from all Pownce members. The service was never launched, but it gives some insight into how Pownce was intending to expand the file-sharing part of its offering.

FIGURE 6.6
Pundits noticed Pownce's ever-decreasing traffic, as indicated in this graph that jokingly referred to the popular TechCrunch technology news site.

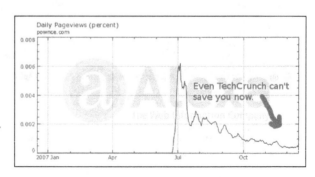

FIGURE 6.7

The never-launched Pownce.FM, designed to be a crowd-sourced
music-sharing service.

Twitter customers were also hungry to mash-up microblogging data with
data from other services. As in the Pownce situation, external developers
began to create programs that "scraped" data from the Twitter website,
and they even developed a rogue API. Twitter acknowledged the demand
by releasing an official API in September 2006, only two months after
going live. External companies and developers integrated Twitter data
with virtually every device, website, and service around, which in turn
attracted new visitors to Twitter in an accelerated wave of activity.

Twitter kept the front end simple and focused on improving its servers and back-end software to handle the ever-increasing traffic. Its
more robust API encouraged third parties to create plenty of apps and
services. Twitter sacrificed short-term control over what apps were created, but also avoided the risk inherent in those new ventures. Twitter
let other developers take that risk, waited to see which were successful,

then acquired the ones that were complementary to its business. Only later, after becoming the undisputed microblogging leader, did Twitter add Pownce-like features such as photo uploading and group lists.

Twitter's tendency to wait and see also played out in the content. When Twitter's members wanted to tag their posts, they adopted the # symbol. When they wanted to respond to others they adopted the @ symbol. After this usage emerged in the content, Twitter built official features around them.

By 2009 Twitter was so instrumental to worldwide communication that when antigovernment protests erupted in Iran, the U.S. State Department asked Twitter to delay bringing the service down for maintenance in order to support Iranian free speech.[12]

Quantitative Results

In the months following Pownce's launch, traffic declined and plateaued at about 100,000 visits per month (Figure 6.8). The disparity in the number of customers compared to Twitter, along with a general economic meltdown in the United States, contributed to Pownce's decision to shut down the service in December 2008 and sell the assets to another company.

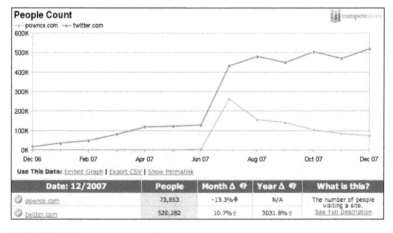

FIGURE 6.8
Monthly visitors to Twitter and Pownce. When Pownce launched publicly in June 2007, it received almost twice the number of visitors as Twitter's best month to date. However, Twitter's traffic jumped at the same time, probably because the Pownce launch attracted attention to microblogging in general.

During 2008 Twitter exploded in popularity, with the number of visitors growing 752 percent over 2007. The service had more than a million visits in March 2008 and more than three million in October 2008 (Figure 6.9). By 2012 Twitter supported hundreds of millions of customers, thousands of tweets per second, and billions of search queries per day.

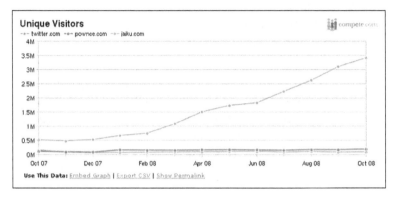

FIGURE 6.9

Twitter's traffic lead created network value that continuously contributed to its growth.

Lessons

Pownce had more features, more rapid feature development, and a prettier visual design. It was more stable and generally well-regarded by customers and the media. How could it lose to Twitter? One explanation is that by the time Pownce launched, Twitter was already the 800-pound gorilla of microblogs, both popular and focused on growth. Pownce came to the game with too little and too late to compete. But unraveling the hows and whys of this story reveals other fascinating lessons.

Positioning Is in the Eye of the Beholder

Pownce bet that creating a unique product with more group-oriented features differentiated its service enough that it didn't need to compete head-to-head with Twitter, in the same way that Twitter can coexist with Facebook. Pownce staff themselves said they weren't competing with Twitter. A comparison of feature sets makes the two seem like different products, and Pownce's plans for music sharing would have further differentiated it. But at its heart Pownce was about microblogging, and most reports from the time rejected this notion of Pownce being different from Twitter, lumping them together as competitors. Positioning, like beauty, is in the eye of the beholder. And once the public considered them equals, it all came down to which social network offered more network value.

Twitter focused directly on growth. The company employed the classic "crossing-the-chasm" tactic of recruiting early adopters first and then, once it achieved momentum, launching an API to further fuel growth, even at the expense of a stable back end.

A valuable lesson can be taken from the fact that customers tolerated Twitter's downtime. In the beginning, Twitter wasn't so critical to anyone's life that downtime was a real problem, and the value of Twitter's size made it interesting enough to tolerate the occasional inconvenience. The appeal of Pownce's superior reliability, features, and visual design wasn't enough to overcome Twitter's size advantage.

Let Them In

Twitter also grew simply by *letting customers in*. The company began with a short internal testing period to develop the service followed by a completely public launch that allowed anyone to join. A similar example is Google+, which launched in 2011 after a restricted public beta period of just a few weeks before opening up to everyone. Pownce's months-long invitation-only period was simply too long and constricted its audience.

Twitter's rate of growth didn't rise dramatically until after Pownce was already in the market. Pownce had the demand to keep up with Twitter, but the invitation-only policy did the opposite by keeping early adopters out.

Funding

Maybe Pownce could have let customers in if they had received more funding. The amount of funding a company has—particularly a start-up—ultimately affects the customers' experience. Pownce's modest initial investment made sense because it had a revenue model that could sustain the company. But as a social media service in a competitive market, growth of the network was more critical than short-term revenue. Twitter's significant venture capital funding meant that it didn't need to worry about generating short-term revenue and could focus on building the necessary back-end capability to handle its traffic. Cash in the bank also gave Twitter the luxury of acquiring successful third-party services rather than run many risky experiments of its own.

Pownce did more of its own customer-facing work, including desktop and iPhone applications. This approach gave the company more control over how these apps were designed, but consumed the available time of its small team, restricting the amount of apps and services that could be created. The system included advertising, Pro Accounts, and group features that required more security, resulting in more complexity. From the perspective of a business model, the feature-rich design and the need to create a large network is a bad match for a modest-revenue model.

Summary

What it was: Pownce was a microblogging and file-sharing service launched in June 2007. Members could choose to post content publicly or only within specific groups. The company accepted a small seed investment. The service had an estimated 100,000 active members. It closed in December 2008.

Why the experience failed: Compared to Twitter, its key competitor, Pownce had richer features, a better visual design, and its system was more stable. But it was harder to sign up for Pownce. And Pownce wasn't integrated into other channels such as mobile as soon or as thoroughly as Twitter.

The underlying cause: Although Pownce tried to differentiate itself, the service was positioned close enough to Twitter that the two became competitors. Pownce had insufficient funding to fuel growth-oriented projects such as building a high-capacity service or promptly building a robust API. Twitter quickly amassed more network value and became the default microblogging service.

The lesson: If your strategic plan relies on a differentiated position, test your product design with your customers to find out if *they* think the product is significantly different. If you're competing for network value, being first to market and focusing on customer acquisition may be more important than extra features, visual design, or even uptime.

Do the Right Thing

"Don't be evil" is . . . a bit of a jab at a lot of the other companies, especially our competitors, who at the time, in our opinion, were kind of exploiting the users to some extent.

—Paul Buchheit, Google[1]

B
usiness scammers and conmen are nothing new, but in the digital world, scams have taken on new forms. As technology and digital business have evolved, these forms have begun to come into focus so we can more clearly identify them and know what it means to do the right thing.

By "do the right thing" I mean the ethical thing: create services that go beyond merely meeting the legal letter of the law and are based on personal moral standards and professional codes of conduct. In the Western world we have a common understanding of professional ethics. For example, the European Union enforces 10 principles for consumer protection, which include "Contracts should be fair to consumers" (number 5) and "Consumers should not be misled" (number 8).

The U.S. Federal Trade Commission lists as its first strategic goal to "Protect Consumers: Prevent fraud, deception, and unfair business practices in the marketplace."

AIGA, the professional design association that dates to 1914, felt the need to go much further and published the AIGA Design Business and Ethics series to explicitly outline what designers must do. Here is an excerpt from "AIGA Standards of Professional Practice":

> A professional designer shall avoid projects that will result in harm to the public. A professional designer shall communicate the truth in all situations and at all times; his or her work shall not make false claims nor knowingly misinform. A professional designer shall represent messages in a clear manner in all forms of communication design and avoid false, misleading and deceptive promotion. A professional designer shall respect the dignity of all audiences and shall value individual differences even as they avoid depicting or stereotyping people or groups of people in a negative or dehumanizing way. A professional designer shall strive to be sensitive to cultural values and beliefs and engages in fair and balanced communication design that fosters and encourages mutual understanding.[2]

You might think such specific guidance would make it clear what designers should do or not do, yet it's not always that easy. Technology and business practices in the digital world change constantly, and as people experience them, their expectations of what is acceptable changes. For example, what constitutes privacy online is a moving target, even for the largest, most experienced companies. In 2007 Facebook released its Beacon feature, which would track customers' use of external shopping websites and use that data to update people's newsfeeds and advertisements. Facebook hoped people would like seeing implicit shopping recommendations from friends, and it constituted a novel form of advertising for partners. Beacon would create messages such as, "Victor bought the movie *American Gigolo* on Fandango," something I may not have wanted to share. Customers thought it was an invasion of privacy, revolted, and started a class action lawsuit. The company later killed the feature and the CEO admitted it was a mistake.

Facebook had problems with privacy again in 2009 when it simplified privacy controls for its 350 million customers, making information such as lists of friends publicly accessible. Facebook had hoped to continue to expand the essence of what made the site successful—information sharing. But customers complained loudly and the company started to roll back the changes within 24 hours.

Both incidents received wide media coverage, but in both cases the company listened closely to customers' complaints and made the necessary changes to keep customers happy.

What follows are two stories of companies that ignored customers' bad experiences for far too long. The first succumbed to unethical temptations, failing customers and itself as a business. The second eventually took the cotton out of its ears and sought redemption, resulting in happier customers and a successful business outcome. Giving up these wicked ways can mean a hard decision to give up easy money and risk business failure. And as we'll see, taking the high road isn't always as easy or as clear as making a decision to sacrifice some revenue.

Classmates.com

A precious few online experiences stand out as truly exciting. Personally, I remember the first time I won an auction on eBay, the first time I clicked *sell* on a profitable online stock trade, and—while still in school back in 1993—e-mailing a famous researcher in my field and receiving a thoughtful reply.

The early days of Classmates.com stand as one of the Web's most powerful, positive customer experiences. Classmates is a social network that helps people find and contact friends and acquaintances from school, work, and the military (Figure 7.1). It was one of the first social media websites and the first to achieve a large-scale audience. Founded in 1995 by Randy Conrads, it dominated the market well before Friendster, MySpace, Facebook, and Twitter emerged. Early on, the company received $15 million in venture capital, turning profitable by 1998 through the sales of advertising and memberships. By 2002 Classmates was one of the most popular sites on the Web.

FIGURE 7.1
The Classmates.com home page as it appeared in April 1997.

The Design

Classmates pioneered many Web design and marketing practices that later became common. Visitors to the site could search for people they know and create a profile for free (Figure 7.2). The company employed a clever permission-marketing technique that alternately revealed information about visitors' acquaintances while asking for personal information, enticing people with the information they wanted while also populating the database with information that could be used to share with other people.

FIGURE 7.2

Viewing a list of students for a particular high school on Classmates.com.

When people found an old classmate they wanted to contact, they would have to buy a subscription to the service to send a message through the website. The subscription price in 2002 was $36 per year.

The Experience

The experience of using Classmates could be highly emotional. As David Evans, a former employee, wrote,

> I remember sitting next to participants in usability interviews as they found their city, school, and friends' names. Their emotion was real when they said, "Wow they're in here?" referring to either a person or school that had once meant a lot to them. That emotion is critical to the success of an online venture. It's similar to what game developers have to see in their playtests; what they call "fiero" the Italian word for fist-pumping triumph. For Classmates, it was the flush of time travel, the rush of memories activated. Without that emotion, no social media or gaming venture can succeed.

Other people I interviewed while working there grew up in rural areas whose graduating classes of no more than 20 had scattered to the wind, or more accurately, migrated to the cities. Lost. Or would be except for this site. Those participants called Classmates an "essential service" in helping them to stitch together their frayed communities.[3]

The Competition

Other social networking sites tried to compete with Classmates in the early days. SixDegrees, for example, started in 1997 and gained some momentum but lacked the emotional draw of finding old friends and folded in 2001.

Friendster, which launched in 2002, was more successful because it offered a subtle way for people to find dates. Three million people signed up the first year and the site was promoted in articles in *Time*, *Esquire*, and *Vanity Fair*. But Friendster failed to scale the service to handle its massive growth, so many people turned instead to MySpace. Founded in 2003, MySpace emphasized music, pop culture, and games, attracting famous musicians who created profiles and posted free music downloads.

In 2004 Facebook launched, originally as a way for university students to connect with other people at their school. It expanded to include high schools in 2005 and in 2006 opened to anyone over the age of 13. In 2007 Facebook launched its app platform, going beyond merely connecting people to becoming a place to shop, play games, and engage with friends in richer ways.

All of these competitors, particularly Facebook, posed a direct threat to Classmates because they gave away similar content for free. Classmates had to act aggressively to compete.

Reactions and Evolution

Early in Classmates' history the powerful customer experience fueled a revenue stream of paying subscribers. This income probably helped the company weather the bursting of the dot-com bubble starting in 2000. Furthermore, the economic recession may have helped Classmates afford to buy so many of the ads that were ubiquitous across the Web at the time (Figure 7.3).

She's a model now?!

Find your high school:

– City –

– State –

Search

Find out what your old High School Friends are up to.

Find Friends

FIGURE 7.3

A classic early Classmates.com online advertisement of the kind that ran between 1997 and 2003. A fun bit of trivia: this is a high school photo of Classmates employee L. A. Smith.

Over the course of 2002 and 2003, Classmates became the fourth most visited site on the Internet. By 2004, 38 million people had registered on the site, and the business had revenue of $54 million, the majority of which came from 1.4 million paying members.

In 2004 the founder sold the company for $100 million to United Online, a larger company that owned Internet service providers NetZero and Juno. Within two years of the sale, the customer experience took a downturn. For example, in 2006 Tom Spring of *PCWorld* conducted a test to find out how easy or difficult it was to cancel a subscription at several different websites. Classmates (and, incidentally, NetZero) ranked among the worst:

> I couldn't find any information on how to cancel until I entered the word *cancel* in the site's search engine. Classmates.com spokesperson John Uppendahl confirmed that there is no other way to find cancellation information. . . .

> Classmates.com also forced me to click through several Web pages reminding me of the benefits I'd lose. Finally my clicking ended at a generic Member Support e-mail contact page containing a blank "Your Question" field. Though the form said nothing about cancellations, I used it to request that the service cancel my subscription. The next day I received an e-mail message confirming that the service had accepted my request.

When I asked Uppendahl why canceling my account took so many steps, he replied that this was the way that Classmates.com handled cancellations. He declined to answer further questions.

Like a number of other services, Classmates.com continued to send me commercial e-mail even after I had unsubscribed from its service.[4]

Around this time, the tone of Classmates' advertising changed as well. Instead of the fun, nostalgic yearbook photos of earlier ads, the new ads used creepy text seemingly targeted at stalkers (Figure 7.4).

FIGURE 7.4
A 2005 ad for Classmates.com.

By 2007 there were plenty of complaints in online forums about the site's billing practices, and the Federal Trade Commission (FTC) opened an investigation into Classmates' automatically renewing subscriptions.

In mid-2007 the Classmates subsidiary of United Online filed its intention to go public and raise up to $144 million, while still retaining majority ownership in the company. Stock analysts were bearish, citing the FTC probe. Analysts also pointed out that customer engagement with the site was low; after the initial rush of finding old friends, Classmates didn't offer much reason to return to the site. Betsy Schiffman, reporting for *Wired*, wrote, "We're not billionaire investors here, but we'd rather buy a $12 hot dog than a share of Classmates.com."[5]

In December 2007 Classmates canceled the initial public offering, signaling a lack of interest from investors. In an interesting coincidence, the FTC ended its probe the *same day*, without taking action against the company.

In November 2008 a class action lawsuit was filed against Classmates for fraudulent e-mail marketing. The lead plaintiff claimed he received e-mails that said old friends were viewing his profile and trying to contact him, and that to contact these friends he would have to upgrade to a paid membership for $15. In reality, the people visiting the plaintiff's profile were general Classmates members, not old friends. The deception inherent in this campaign plays on the very strong emotional draw that is at the core of the Classmates customer experience (Figure 7.5). Classmates denied wrongdoing, but agreed to pay up to $9.5 million to the more than three million people who signed up for the service after seeing these e-mails.

FIGURE 7.5

This e-mail from Classmates from 2009 is an example of a less personal format following the 2008 fraudulent e-mail marketing lawsuit.

The initial legal settlement offered each claimant only $3, or a $2 credit for the site. A U.S. district court judge rejected this settlement as inadequate, later approving another that awarded each claimant up to $15.

The lawsuit further besmirched Classmates' reputation to the point where the media felt comfortable brazenly attacking the company (Figure 7.6).

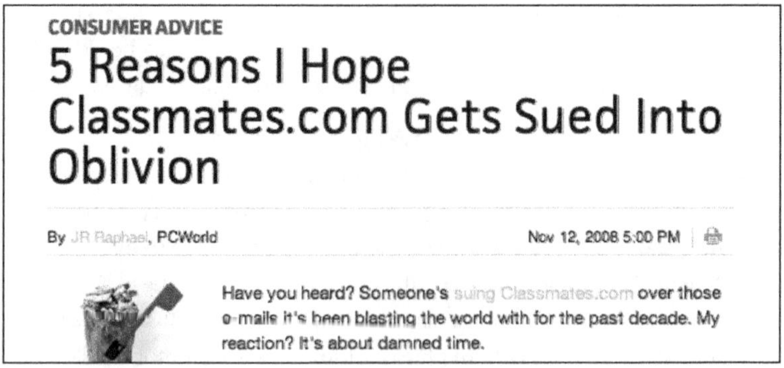

CONSUMER ADVICE

5 Reasons I Hope Classmates.com Gets Sued Into Oblivion

By JR Raphael, PCWorld Nov 12, 2008 5:00 PM

Have you heard? Someone's suing Classmates.com over those e-mails it's been blasting the world with for the past decade. My reaction? It's about damned time.

FIGURE 7.6
By 2008 it wasn't unusual for publications such as *PCWorld* to boldly criticize Classmates.

In November 2009 the U.S. Senate attacked three Internet marketing companies and their partners, including Classmates, for post-transaction marketing practices, or "piggybacking." In a piggybacking scheme, additional services are added to a customer's bill during the checkout process without the customer realizing it. In some cases credit card information was even transferred to a third party without the customer's permission. The additional services were usually of dubious value, such as "cash-back rewards" that were never delivered and for which customers were charged on a monthly basis. The only way customers would find out that the transactions occurred was if they checked their credit card bills. One of the Internet marketing companies, Webloyalty, acknowledged that, "at least 90 percent of our members don't know anything about the membership."[6] Classmates made more than $70 million with this tactic.

In August 2010 the New York attorney general conducted a similar investigation and reached a settlement with the marketing companies and their partners. The largest fine for a partner company was to Classmates for $960,000.

In January 2010 Classmates announced it would make profile information publicly accessible on Facebook, the iPhone, and other places, marking a change from its previous practice of making profiles available only to paying members. The move was seen as a way to compete with Facebook and other social media sites that were free and allowed easier access to content. Classmates' customers, perceiving this as an unfair and deceptive change in privacy practices, filed a lawsuit against the company later that year. Classmates denied wrongdoing, but settled the lawsuit for $2.5 million.

Quantitative Results

By 2011 what was once a top site on the Web was now the 4,211th most visited website. Traffic was flat for years, revenue started to decline in 2009, and between 2010 and 2011 paid accounts declined. United Online announced in early 2011 it would fold the Classmates site into another new site called Memory Lane, which offers nostalgic content such as high school yearbooks, movie trailers, music, and photographs.

For at least a few months in 2011 the classmates.com domain redirected to memorylane.com, with the Classmates functions available from there. But within months Classmates.com was back online (Figure 7.7).

FIGURE 7.7

The Classmates.com home page as it appeared in 2012.

Plaxo

Plaxo is an online address book that tries to alleviate a pain that was common in the early 2000s: keeping online address book information up to date across a person's computers, phones, PDAs, and Web services such as Web-based e-mail (Figure 7.8). Plaxo was started in November 2002 with a $3.8 million venture capital investment. The basic service was free. In 2005 Plaxo added a $50 per year Premium plan that included mobile access, automatic consolidation of duplicate entries, and customer support.

FIGURE 7.8
The Plaxo public home page, 2011.

The Design

Plaxo essentially synchronized contact information between people, devices, and services. If one of your friends updated her address on Plaxo, that change would be reflected in your Plaxo address book. Plaxo would also update the address book on your computer and smartphone. And it could import contacts from services such as LinkedIn (Figure 7.9). You can watch a video demonstration of Plaxo at http://rfld.me/VJR2bb.

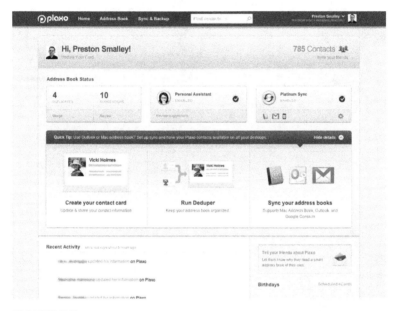

FIGURE 7.9
A customer's Plaxo home page, 2011.

For our purposes, the feature that is most relevant involves *non-customers*. Let's say you don't use Plaxo but your friend Joe does and he has you in his address book. Plaxo would send you an e-mail saying, "Can you update your contact information for Joe?" Plaxo would send these "update request" e-mails periodically for every one of Joe's friends who didn't use Plaxo. Unlike other online services that contact you once you sign up, Plaxo contacted you more when you *didn't* sign up, asking you to do work to power the service.

The Experience

The Plaxo customer experience was straightforward: install the software, learn how to use it, and manage your contacts. A significant number of customers loved that Plaxo sent update request e-mails to their contacts who weren't customers because it meant much of the address book maintenance was automated (Figure 7.10).

FIGURE 7.10
A Plaxo update request e-mail.

But a lot of the non-customers thought this was a giant, annoying waste of their time. Non-customers received so many e-mails from Plaxo that they considered it spam. Jeff Nolan, a venture capitalist and blogger, related a typical experience: "I hate that service because once I unwittingly spammed my entire contact database that I had uploaded years ago simply by updating my contact information."[7]

Plaxo tried to alleviate the pain caused by update request e-mails. The company let recipients opt out, though the opt-out form on the website was hard to find. If you wanted to opt out you needed to go through several steps: fill out a form on one screen, confirm that you want to opt out on another screen, then go to your e-mail program to look for a confirmation e-mail from Plaxo and click the confirmation button in the message. And if Plaxo was sending e-mails to more than one of your e-mail addresses, you had to go though this entire process for each address.

It's easy to find complaints about Plaxo in the blogs and forums of the time. Sentiment analysis of Plaxo on the Internet was 73 percent hate versus 27 percent love.[8] By 2006 Plaxo had about 10 million customers, and if we estimate that each of those customers had 100 contacts in their address book, Plaxo could have been sending out hundreds of millions of update requests.

Reactions

When Plaxo was new, reactions from the media were positive. In March 2003 Russell Glitman of *PC Magazine* wrote, "Recipients get an e-mail with your contact information and theirs. They add any missing information, correct errors, and send the form back. The process is simple and effective."[9]

But by December 2003 the frustration with the sheer volume of update request e-mails grew to the point that journalists, venture capitalists, and A-list bloggers publicly criticized Plaxo as well. David Coursey at ZDNet wrote, "I don't respond to Plaxo requests, won't join Plaxo, and recommend you don't, either."[10] Michael Arrington at TechCrunch wrote, "[A]s we are forced to deal with Plaxo spam and various avoidance processes, we are told by them that the best way to avoid the spam is to simply become a member of Plaxo. . . . It's like a stalker telling his stalkee that if she will only marry him, he'll stop."[11] Jeff Nolan called Plaxo's approach "the 'Piss Off Your Prospects Enough That They Sign Up' sales model."

Plaxo's response to this media backlash was to defend themselves, vigorously attacking the attackers. For example, at one point Arrington called attention to Plaxo's aggressive public relations tactics: "Plaxo has a reputation for releasing the attack dogs whenever they are slammed online. I made the mistake of voicing my opinion on an old . . . post. By the end of the exchange I wished I had never started."[12] In response to this piece he got an earful from Plaxo's privacy officer. Arrington, exhausted, finally responded, "I surrender."

The Competition

Plaxo's main competition was GoodContacts, founded in 2000 (Figure 7.11). It functioned similarly, but two key differences set Plaxo apart. One is that the Plaxo software installed on a Windows PC could tightly integrate with the Microsoft Outlook e-mail client. Without leaving Outlook, you could use a Plaxo toolbar to edit and send your outgoing contact information or create new contacts (Figure 7.12).

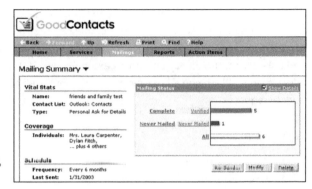

FIGURE 7.11
Plaxo's key competitor,
GoodContacts, 2003.

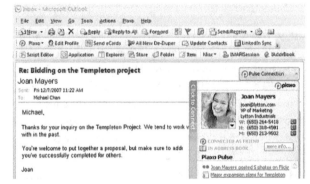

FIGURE 7.12
The Plaxo toolbar for
Microsoft Outlook
helped people manage
contacts from within
their e-mail software.

The other innovation was that Plaxo went beyond software you installed on your PC to become what we now call a cloud-based service. Contact information was stored on Plaxo's centralized servers so that when people updated their information, it could be updated in other Plaxo customers' address books. Operating from centralized servers later enabled Plaxo to offer mobile Web access, too. And notably the servers also sent and received update request e-mails. This infrastructure was key to enabling growth on a larger scale than was possible before.

GoodContacts was acquired by Reunion.com for $5 million in 2004 and then faded from popularity.

Evolution

Over the course of 2005 and 2006, Plaxo added more features, such as the ability to import contacts from LinkedIn. But the update request e-mails continued.

Internally, Plaxo leadership debated whether to continue sending update requests.[13] Those in favor argued that customers loved the effectiveness of the update request e-mails, and although some non-customers found them annoying, the e-mails were a vital source of viral growth for the company. To abandon the feature would eliminate a core part of the value proposition and stall growth.

The argument against was championed by people such as John McCrea, vice president of marketing, who predicted that the growing frustration with update requests among non-customers and the media would inflict long-term damage to the Plaxo brand.[14] Damage to the brand could harm Plaxo's ability to acquire customers and possibly even the company's attractiveness as an acquisition target. By this time Plaxo had accepted approximately $20 million in venture capital, and these investors were probably looking forward to either an acquisition or an initial public offering that would yield a suitable return on their investment.

The argument against prevailed, and in March 2006 Plaxo management announced they would start to retire the use of update requests.

> We are no longer aggressively pushing new users to send out e-mails and are adding restrictions to prevent existing users from sending out large batches. Within the next six months (allowing for releases and upgrades to our base), you should see these messages drop to a trickle.[15]

In response, journalist Michael Arrington responded, "So overall, I'm happy that Plaxo is doing this and I applaud them for it. But how about an official apology as well? *Nevermind, they'd just send it by email anyway.*"[16]

A few days later, Plaxo's CEO accepted the challenge and offered an apology on the company blog (Figure 7.13), although he stopped short of actually admitting wrongdoing.

To everyone who hated getting Plaxo update messages, felt we were generating acquaintance spam, or otherwise were harmed by the service, I personally apologize on behalf of all of the people at Plaxo. I know we have a long way to go to earn your trust, and can only ask that you judge us by our actions going forward.[17]

FIGURE 7.13

The apology published on Plaxo's blog was signed by the company's CEO, Ben Golub, and included an illustration of flying pigs. At least Plaxo had a sense of humor.

As predicted, some existing customers were upset when they lost the update request feature, but the media hailed the decision as a giant step in the right direction. Plaxo was now growing at the rate of 50,000 new customers a day, and the company believed it had enough momentum to reduce the update requests. Instead management looked to product design for ways to keep address books updated. Over time they added automated, multidirectional synchronization of contacts and calendars among the major Internet sites such as Google and Yahoo! and for both PC and Mac software. They created the Plaxo Personal Assistant, which searches the Internet for contact data, cleans it up, and offers it as an update. And somewhat ironically they rolled out a feature called Card-Sharing that flips the update request on its head by offering the contact information of Plaxo members to the people in their address book.

Quantitative Results

After dumping the update requests, Plaxo was still attractive enough to investors to receive a $9 million infusion in early 2007, for a total investment of more than $28 million. By the spring of 2008 Plaxo had 20 million customers and had grown to more than two million unique visitors a month, doubling the previous year's traffic. Plaxo was acquired by Comcast in 2008 for a significant sum, said to be in the $150 million to $170 million range. As of 2013, the service was still active.

Lessons

Both Classmates and Plaxo use what I call the "free-content/recurring-billing" business model. Customers create the content (e.g., profiles or contact information, respectively) and the business charges them a subscription to access that collection of content. Plenty of businesses that depend on customer-generated content, from LinkedIn to Match.com, use the very same business model.

The subscription fee is charged month after month, and inevitably some of these customers will become "sleepers" who stop using the service but forget to cancel their subscriptions. Businesses that are less ethical will (oops) forget to wake them up. And so it shouldn't be surprising that this business model tempts businesses down a slippery slope of unethical behavior. I know some companies dance on the line between ethical and unethical marketing and billing practices because I've been there and I've seen it. When I encounter a service, such as Flickr, that by default *stops* billing you at the end of the billing cycle unless you opt in, I'm not sure whether to praise the company for its pro-customer stance or fault it for making its business less financially sustainable. Not even the non-profit, pro-customer *Consumer Reports* goes that far.

The business model isn't inherently evil, as services like Flickr demonstrate. Ethical businesses find some other competitive advantage to become profitable. They might offer lower prices, though the Internet drives down prices in general, making it difficult to compete on price. More often the product is differentiated through good design and marketing.

Staying Ethical through Good Design

Classmates went from good to bad to irrelevant; Plaxo went from bad to good to successful. The reasons behind those transitions are valuable lessons.

Both services started with databases hungry for content. Classmates could have been overly aggressive from the start, but didn't need to. The emotional appeal of finding old friends was enough to encourage people to join and create a profile.

For all the initial appeal of Classmates, there wasn't much to keep people using and paying for the service. The company started to facilitate reunions, but reunions don't occur frequently enough to generate much revenue. Facebook solved this problem with its stream of updates that keep people returning to see what's new with their friends and family. Classmates could have turned to designers to develop engaging features like this before, or at least in reaction to, Facebook's dominance, but instead the company spent its resources elsewhere. Classmates squandered a giant first-mover advantage. Maybe Facebook would have won anyway, but at least Classmates could have tried copying features from Facebook, just as Facebook copied the status updates feature from Twitter.

Classmates suffered customer experience and business failure. Reasons for this failure include legal troubles, low customer engagement, a failure to go public, damage to the brand, and intense competition from Facebook. All but the last was of its management's own doing.

Unfortunately for customers, frustrating businesses like this can profit for years if they provide just enough value with just enough ethics. But that's a lonely road, a road investors may not want to travel. Classmates failed to go public, which meant no big payday for the executive management. Good riddance.

Plaxo started with a similar challenge: filling the database. Although the idea of an automatically updated address book is appealing, it doesn't carry quite the emotional intensity of finding old friends. So Plaxo initially had to resort to more aggressive methods. To be fair, competitor GoodContacts also sent out potentially annoying update request e-mails, but not at anything near the volume that Plaxo did.

Because Plaxo eventually turned off the update requests, one could argue that the ends (eventual customer experience and business success) justified the means (an annoying experience for a lot of people). But only important matters such as health or security justify a bad experience for so many people. Besides, consider the opportunity cost that Plaxo paid by becoming a toxic brand. The company might have become much bigger. Instead of 20 million customers, it might have had hundreds of millions. Instead of becoming just a business unit within Comcast, Plaxo could have become a ubiquitous part of the Internet infrastructure, the de facto standard for managing contact information. This is, potentially, what we all lost.

Blowing Whistles

For a long time the Plaxo founders, investors, and executives held a positive view of their methods.[18] They had found a way to solve the problem of easily updated contact information and do it on the scale of tens of millions of people. The service was new, effective, and popular, the very definition of an innovation.

Up until the time that it stopped the update requests, the company didn't have an in-house marketing person and its management had been described as "tone deaf" to the complaints around them. It wasn't until the consistent high-profile criticism of journalists such as Michael Arrington began that Plaxo started to consider what long-term damage it was doing to the brand.

Still, management faced a dilemma. The update request e-mails were valuable to current customers, served a marketing function to popularize Plaxo, and therefore brought in revenue. Should they end the e-mails and face an uncertain future just to please the media and people who were *not* customers? Without the update requests they faced a risky short-term future, and with the update requests they faced a risky long-term future.

To push a company from the dark side to the light side, one or more individuals need to argue persuasively for this point of view, to be the moral force that convinces others to do the right thing. You may have experienced this situation when you or someone on your team took the initiative to point out the ethical problems with a course of business. This task isn't easy and it's often uncomfortable. In Plaxo's case, people like John McCrea did the difficult work of advocating for customers and the brand, and won. Thank you.

Summary

Classmates.com

What it is: Classmates.com is a social network to help people find and contact friends and acquaintances from school, work, and the military. It was founded in 1995, received $15 million in venture capital, and by 2002 was one of the most popular sites on the Web. By 2004 the site had 38 million customer accounts, 10.3 million paid subscribers, and more than $50 million in annual revenue. That same year the founder sold the company for $100 million to United Online. By 2010 traffic to the site had declined so dramatically that in 2011 the site content and functions were folded into another site.

Why the experience failed: Starting around 2006, customers began accusing the company of many anticonsumer practices, including an obstructive subscription cancellation process, deceptive tactics for automatically renewing subscriptions, fraudulent e-mail marketing, fraudulent credit card charges, and deceptive privacy practices. Classmates paid millions of dollars to settle class action lawsuits.

The underlying cause: A series of unethical and possibly illegal marketing, billing, and privacy practices hurt the brand and sidestepped serious attempts to innovate, allowing competitor Facebook to steal the market with free content and compelling features.

The lesson: Good design can be a more ethical, productive, and financially sustainable way to attract customer engagement than unethical business practices.

Plaxo

What it is: Plaxo is an online, automatically updating address book service launched in 2002. As of May 2008 Plaxo had 20 million customers. More than $28 million was invested in the company, and in 2008 it was acquired by Comcast for somewhere between $150 and $170 million.

Why the experience failed: Plaxo aggressively e-mailed many non-customers to solicit updates to their contact information, frustrating many people in the process, and ultimately gaining a reputation as a spammer. After prominent journalists shone light on the problem, Plaxo's management team redeemed itself by shutting off the offensive e-mails.

The underlying cause: The Plaxo "update request" e-mails began harmlessly enough and were comparable to a competitor's techniques. But the e-mails were increased to such a staggering volume that they far exceeded customer expectations of the day. Because the problem surfaced gradually, Plaxo management was largely unaware of the customer experience problem until journalists attacked them and hurt the brand.

The lesson: Redemption is possible if employees persuasively argue for the strategic value of a positive customer experience. Because companies are to some extent insulated from the effects of their actions, they need to stay aware of their customers' experience to ensure they are acting ethically.

CHAPTER 8

Cannibalize
Yourself

> If you don't cannibalize yourself, someone else will.

> —Steve Jobs

P roducts constantly hold a tension between stasis and change. In business there is tension between selling what you created to obtain a return on your investment and creating new products to increase future profits. For customers there is tension between the easy reliability of the familiar product that has already been paid for and the thrill of the new and improved product that costs more money.

For designers there is always dissatisfaction with the shortcomings of what we have now, a constant burning desire to push forward to create something better.

Here are the stories of two products whose tension between stasis and change pushed them in two different directions, both of which disappointed customers. The first, Symbian, didn't change fast enough and forfeited a €100 billion industry leadership position. The second, Final Cut Pro X, changed so fast it enraged customers, then later redeemed itself.

Symbian

In March 2012 Symbian was more popular worldwide than any mobile phone operating system in the world, measured by the phones people actually had in their pockets. Since its inception, manufacturers have sold close to 400 million Symbian-powered mobile devices. And yet by 2012 Symbian was already close to death. According to sources that worked at Nokia at the time, watching a company grow to dominate an entire industry and then fail within the span of a few short years was a completely surreal experience.

Engineer Fredrik Idestam established Nokia as a paper manufacturer in 1865. Around the turn of the 20th century, Nokia employed its industrial expertise to expand into electricity generation, electrical cables, and rubber products. In the 1960s the company expanded into electronics and produced a wide range of commercial and consumer products, including telecommunications equipment. Nokia helped develop the first car phone in 1982 (Figure 8.1) and launched its first mobile phone in 1984. Soon this was the fastest-growing segment of the company. Throughout the 1990s Nokia divested itself of other businesses to focus on telecommunications, and became known worldwide as the largest manufacturer of mobile phones.

Nokia's engineering genealogy is visible in the hardware expertise it brings to mobile phone design. For example, in 1998 Nokia engineers realized they could hide the bulky, seven-inch mobile phone antenna by stamping a thin piece of metal and shaping it to fit inside the phone. The outside of the phone was then designed to be held in a way that would prevent people from covering the antenna and blocking the signal (Figure 8.2). The entire industry followed Nokia's lead.[1]

FIGURE 8.1
Nokia helped develop the Mobira Senator in 1982, one of the first car phones in the world.

FIGURE 8.2
The Nokia 8810, the first mobile phone to hide the antenna inside the case.

Nokia also mastered variant manufacturing—designing and building hundreds of different models to serve different customer segments, technologies, markets, and carriers. In 2007 alone 38 distinct models were released. Some worked on different wireless telecommunication networks around the world. Some were simple, inexpensive phones that sold for $29; others were smartphones that were essentially small computers and cost hundreds of dollars. Some phones specialized in playing music, others in playing games, and some had dedicated keyboards for business users who frequently wrote messages. Other phones featured FM radios, GPS, Wi-Fi, photo and video cameras, and Bluetooth. They supported up to 48 languages. When it came to mobile device hardware expertise, Nokia was second to none.

In the 1990s, mobile phones started to converge with personal digital assistants (PDAs) so that phones could do more than just make calls— they could store names and addresses, calendar events, and play simple games. At that time, companies usually specialized in one or the other: computer-oriented companies like Psion focused on PDAs while tele-communications-oriented companies like Nokia focused on phones. In 1998 Nokia sought to strengthen its position by forming a joint venture with Psion, Ericsson, and Motorola to form Symbian Ltd. The new orga-nization shared the EPOC operating system from the Psion Organizer, which was renamed Symbian OS. Two years later Nokia released its first phone using Symbian, the Nokia 9210 Communicator. By 2002 more than two million Symbian phones had shipped. In 2009 the nonprofit Symbian Foundation assumed development of the OS. Whereas Android has more recently become the dominant mobile operating platform shared among multiple phone manufacturers, Symbian pioneered this role a decade earlier. Symbian-powered devices were released by as many as 10 differ-ent Symbian Foundation member companies.

Symbian represented an innovative advance in embedded operat-ing systems. Most significantly, the software interface platform that Nokia created to work with Symbian, called S60, introduced the abil-ity to install new applications onto the phone, making phones more like personal computers and essentially creating a new category of mobile phones that we now call smartphones.

The Design

For most of its life, the Symbian interface that appeared on feature phones was not remarkably different from the interface of competitors' phones. Home screens had icons that represented applications such as Calendar and Contacts. Applications were largely menu-driven and selections were made with hardware buttons.

In 2008 Nokia released its first S60 touchscreen phones, the 5800 Xpress-Music and the N97. The two phones ran Symbian with a new version of the S60 interface platform called 5th Edition designed for use with touchscreens (Figure 8.3). By building on Symbian and S60, Nokia chose to retain some backward compatibility with its giant established market share, engineer-ing investment, and universe of compatible third-party applications.

Like their predecessors, these phones were feature-rich, and included voice-command recognition, instant messaging, file and application managers, and a 3.2 megapixel camera. You can watch a video review of the N97 at http://rfld.me/12wbHkN.

FIGURE 8.3
A home screen on Symbian S60,
5th Edition.

But even though they arrived almost a year after the iPhone and touch-screen phones from all the other major manufacturers, the 5800 and N97 used resistive touchscreens—old technology that has been offered to consumers since the PalmPilots of the 1990s. Resistive touchscreens are capable of high accuracy, but only when using a stylus. The iPhone and Android phones use a different technology—capacitive touchscreens—that can only be used with fingers but are highly sensitive.

The cases of the 5800 and N97 also revealed Nokia's approach to inter-action. The 5800 came with a stand to hold the phone upright for use with an accompanying stylus (Figure 8.4a). The N97 included a physi-cal keyboard that, when unfolded, positioned the thumbs for typing and selecting options with a d-pad (Figure 8.4b).

FIGURE 8.4a,b
The 5800 XpressMusic was Nokia's first Symbian S60 touchscreen phone, which included the stand and stylus shown here (a). The Nokia N97 included a physical keyboard with a d-pad, a square-shaped pad on the left of the keyboard for selecting items on the screen (b).

The Experience

People who are only familiar with later technology might not see much of a difference between feature phones running Symbian and a competitor's operating system. Each had its own idiosyncrasies, and when people expressed a preference it was usually for the idiosyncrasies of one interface over another. The mobile phone manufacturers generally differentiated their products not with interface design but with industrial design and software-driven features. For example, preferences were strong for flip-phones, phones with a physical keyboard, or phones that were small enough to fit in a pocket.

When Nokia released touchscreen phones, suddenly the experience changed. Some of this change was due to new hardware. Setting the 5800 on the included stand was a natural position for using a stylus but awkward for touching it with fingers because it required positioning the arm at table level and bending the wrist upward. Similarly, unfolding the N97 made it easy to type on the physical keyboard and use the d-pad; however, reaching around the device with an index finger to touch the screen was less comfortable.

The choice of hardware signaled Nokia's position on touchscreen interaction: the stylus had priority over fingers. This stutter step toward touch interaction was more apparent in the software interface, as the media reviews pointed out.

Reactions

The media strongly criticized the touchscreen interface. For example, Chris Ziegler's review of the 5800 for Engadget said,

> If you take a Ferrari and duct-tape a hull to the bottom of it, does it become a speedboat? No, of course it doesn't. Likewise, if you take S60 3.2—a perfectly capable, reasonably usable smartphone platform powering tens of millions of devices around the world—and duct-tape touch support to it, you're not going to end up with a very usable system, and it's bewildering to us that Nokia seems to have thought otherwise. 5th Edition is, for all practical purposes, a remix of 3rd Edition Feature Pack 2 that's been mildly massaged to support touchscreens, and the result is nothing short of a usability nightmare.[2]

Moving from a non-touchscreen interface to a touchscreen means redesigning it so that instead of indirectly manipulating objects on the screen using hardware buttons, you directly manipulate onscreen objects with your fingers. For example, when viewing an image on an older feature phone, there might be a "zoom out" label that corresponds with a physical button on the phone. But on an iPhone or Android phone you simply pinch the image with two fingers to zoom in or out.

The S60 5th Edition didn't fully transition from indirect to direct manipulation; it took one step into the world of touchscreens while leaving one foot behind in the world of button operation. When running an old application that required buttons, a d-pad (a set of buttons for moving up, down, left, or right) would appear on the screen (Figure 8.5). The N97 phone opened to reveal a physical keyboard as well as a physical d-pad control (see Figure 8.4b). An onscreen cursor, which serves no purpose on a touchscreen device, still appeared at times. Some onscreen controls required a single tap or a double tap, with no way to predict which was needed. And there were no touch-specific gestures, such as pinching to zoom in and out of photos.

FIGURE 8.5
A d-pad appears on a Nokia touchscreen, mimicking the physical d-pad of older phones.

As the new flagship smartphone with state-of-the-art features, expectations for the N97 were high. But the same issues were apparent with the N97 as with the 5800, as Vincent Nguyen wrote in *Phone Magazine*:

> It's S60 5th Edition that provides perhaps the biggest usability frustration [with the N97]. Nokia's OS is, in the face of attractive and modern platforms like that [of] the iPhone or Palm's webOS, looking a little visually tired, and the touch enabling they've done feels half-hearted. Not only is there little in the way of visual gloss that users have come to expect, such as screen transitions or animations, but the way touch has been implemented seems an afterthought. There are no gestures or similar controls, instead buttons have merely been made chunkier and menus larger. There's also a slight graininess, which is visible from some angles, which mars an otherwise decent LCD panel with high resolution.[3]

The Competition

In June 2007 Apple released the iPhone (Figure 8.6).

FIGURE 8.6
In 1997 Apple released the iPhone, one of the first phones in the world to feature a capacitive touchscreen.

The reaction from Nokia management, according to my sources who worked at the company at the time, echoed what many in the press said: the iPhone was pretty, but it was barely a real competitor. There was only one model of iPhone, and it lacked many of the features that Nokia's phones offered: the ability to send photos with text messages, custom ringtones, copy and paste, spell-check, wireless audio for Bluetooth headsets, Adobe Flash Player, editing of Microsoft Office documents, voice-activated dialing, video capture, language localization, and customization for network operators. When the rechargeable battery ran out of charges, the iPhone had to be returned to Apple for a new battery.

And yet Apple customers lined up to buy one because they knew that despite the iPhone's lack of features it would offer them a great experience. The phone itself looked beautiful, with optical-grade glass tightly fit within a steel rim and minimal buttons and decoration. The onscreen graphics were colorful and exciting. When you slid your fingers across the touchscreen, the graphics were as responsive as physical objects. You can watch a video review of the first iPhone at http://rfld.me/14UZFkI.

The iPhone was less functional, but it was fun to use. Instead of focusing on features that showed up on a list of specifications, Apple focused on making the phone a delight to interact with. And Apple didn't simply see the touchscreen as a new way to press buttons; it became a conduit for new kinds of interactions, whether panning and zooming through maps or quickly flicking through lists. This was a massive shift in thinking for the mobile phone industry. Nokia's phones did many things well, but the customers' experiences were now focused on the touchscreen.

To appreciate the level of detail Apple pursued when designing the iPhone, look at the simple act of transitioning from one screen to another (Figure 8.7). On the iPhone, screens often appear to slide to the left as a new screen slides in from the right. But John Blackburn, author of the Malt Whisky iPhone app, discovered that sliding screens don't simply slide.[4] Some elements on the screen fade out as they slide out, while others fade in as they slide in. Some elements, such as the new screen title, slide in faster, probably so your eye can read the title and orient you to the new content on the screen. One element, the back arrow button, doesn't slide at all; it just quickly fades in, probably to give you the ready option to navigate back if that's your intention. And the button that you tapped turns a strong blue color and stays this way throughout the animation to make it clear the app received your input. Like an animated cartoon, all this movement happens so quickly that you don't notice it happening, but the end result guides your eye so you can quickly access the controls and read the text in a logical order.

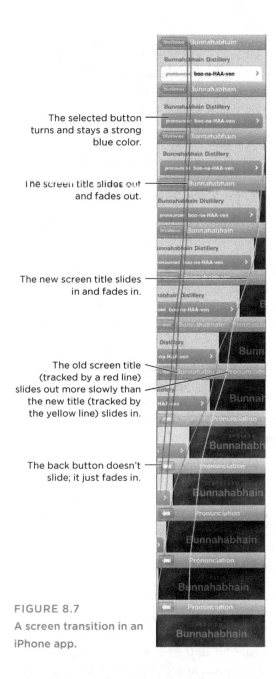

The selected button turns and stays a strong blue color.

The screen title slides out and fades out.

The new screen title slides in and fades in.

The old screen title (tracked by a red line) slides out more slowly than the new title (tracked by the yellow line) slides in.

The back button doesn't slide; it just fades in.

FIGURE 8.7
A screen transition in an iPhone app.

In later versions of Symbian S60, screens faded from one to another, which was elegant but simplistic in comparison to the iPhone. Rotating the phone between landscape and portrait orientations on Symbian could switch the display with an abrupt flash. On the iPhone the orientation transition was a smooth animation.

In late 2007 Google announced its new Android mobile operating system. When the first Android phones reached the market in late 2008, the OS exhibited a different design aesthetic than the iPhone, but it too focused on a robust touchscreen interface (Figure 8.8). One by one, companies in the Symbian Foundation abandoned Symbian for Android. Soon only Nokia was left.

FIGURE 8.8
The HTC Dream, released in 2008, was the first mobile phone to use the Android operating system.

Despite the design shortcomings and mixed reviews in the press, Nokia impressively sold more than 10 million 5800 and N97 phones in 2009, no doubt due to the massive base of existing Nokia customers who simply wanted to upgrade, as well as strong Nokia brand recognition. But that same year, the iPhone claimed 24 million in sales and Android almost 7 million. Within two years the tide had turned.

Evolution

At the end of 2009 Nokia released the X6 phone, a replacement for the 5800. The X6 was Nokia's first capacitive touchscreen phone. The hardware form was now similar to that of its competitors. The X6 made the usual advance in features, including a high-resolution camera with a dual LED flash. Although the X6 used a version of Symbian with usability improvements, the processor was overburdened by the user interface demands. Dave Stevenson wrote on TechRadar:

> Our chief problem with the X6 is its performance. We were often left guessing whether our key press had been recognised, and sometimes tapping a button again resulted in unpredictable behaviour. . . . The extra second or so occasionally encountered between tapping an icon and anything happening is frustrating.[5]

We know from decades of usability research that people feel a system is reacting instantaneously if feedback happens within 0.1 second, and for the flow of thought to stay uninterrupted requires feedback within 1.0 second.[6] So it's not surprising that the experience of extra seconds between tapping and feedback on the X6 was frustrating.

Part of the success of the iPhone and Android phones was the luxury of starting from scratch with a new operating system to suit this new world of touchscreens and Internet connectivity. Nokia's first attempt to start over, Series 90, was killed to reduce costs. A new version of Symbian, Symbian^3, was developed to fix the user interface quirks. But the software was delayed as Nokia kept adding features. When it was ready in 2010 Nokia finally had phones with the robust user interface they should have had years earlier, but it was too late to reverse the sales trend (Figure 8.9).

FIGURE 8.9
Nokia's 808 PureView runs Symbian^3. Launched in 2012, it's likely to be the last Symbian smartphone. In a continuation of Nokia's traditional strengths, the 808's camera features a 41 megapixel, 1″ × 1.2″ sensor, the largest and highest resolution sensor at the time of its release.

A similar fate met another project called Maemo, which was intended to be Nokia's next-generation operating system. Maemo was folded into a joint venture with Intel to become MeeGo. The first MeeGo-powered Nokia device, the N9, didn't arrive on the market until late 2011. The hardware and software were good enough to match the competition, but by this time there were thousands of applications and accessories available for the iPhone and Android phones.

Quantitative Results

Between 2006 and 2010, Symbian's market share plunged from 73 percent to 36 percent. Although Nokia was still the largest mobile device manufacturer by far (Figure 8.10), it was losing the smartphone race, the market segment with the largest profit margins. In 2011 Apple and Google overtook Nokia in shipments of smartphones, and in 2012 Samsung replaced Nokia as the leader in overall mobile phone shipments (Figure 8.11).

In February 2011 Nokia announced it would transition to using Microsoft's Windows Phone as its primary smartphone platform. By July 2012 Nokia captured 59 percent of all Windows Phone sales. But Windows Phone only accounted for less than 3 percent of the overall market.

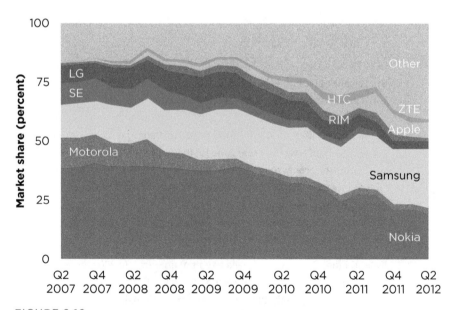

FIGURE 8.10
Market share of mobile phone vendors, 2007–2012.

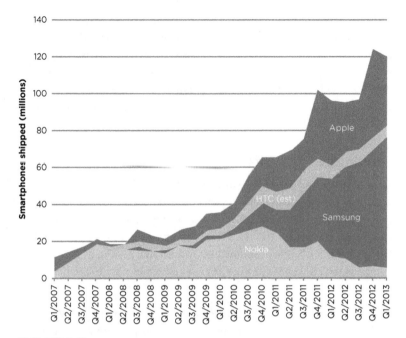

FIGURE 8.11

Number of smartphone units shipped, 2007–2012.

Final Cut Pro X

In 1999 Apple entered the world of professional video editing with the release of its Final Cut Pro software. In a world of difficult-to-use software and awkward hardware configurations, Apple's product streamlined it all. Final Cut didn't require extra hardware for video output or accelerated operations, and it was fast enough to provide some transitions and effects in real time instead of making editors wait while the computer processed the video. It utilized Apple's QuickTime multimedia framework, which has been continuously refined since 1991. For large film projects, Final Cut made it easy for editors to manage thousands of media clips. Overall it was faster and more reliable, and of course it featured Apple's legendary user interface design.

By 2001 Final Cut was being used to edit major films. In 2002 the software won a Primetime Emmy Engineering Award for its impact on the television industry. By 2011 Final Cut accounted for more than half of all video-editing software sales, with a far larger market share than its competition.

In June 2011 Apple released a major new version called Final Cut Pro X (the *X* is pronounced "ten"). Soon after, close to half the reviews on Apple's App Store read like this:

- "Horrible."

- "Furious."

- "A disaster."

- "Heartbreaking."

What could possibly have happened to turn so many customers against a product they loved? It is important to note that many of these customers were video professionals, people who earned their living with their expert ability to use the software. Some of them ran their businesses with Final Cut installed on multiple workstations. They were producers of corporate commercials, special effects experts, and filmmakers, and each had their own unique methods and sets of features they relied on.

The Design

Final Cut Pro X was rebuilt from the ground up as a totally new version, but the initial release didn't include some vital features that professional video editors had come to rely on in previous versions. For example, it lacked the ability to synchronize and edit footage from multiple cameras, export video to video tape, burn more than just basic DVDs, work with file formats from other software, or connect an external video monitor. Worst of all, Final Cut Pro X used a new file format and wouldn't open old Final Cut project files.

The user interface was also redesigned (Figure 8.12). You can watch a video tour of Final Cut Pro X at http://rfld.me/WwAWA6. The new version looked more like Apple's consumer video editing program iMovie, which may have been part of a subtle, long-term strategy to make all Apple software touchscreen-compatible. iMovie, starting with a major new version in 2008, introduced user interface elements and behavior borrowed from the iPhone's iOS touchscreen–oriented software: large regions of content with bigger buttons, full-screen mode, only one file open at a time, and more dragging instead of precise clicking.[7] So it wasn't too surprising that in 2010 iMovie was released for the iPhone and iPad. Perhaps someday Final Cut will also have a touchscreen version.

FIGURE 8.12a,b

A typical screen layout in Final Cut Pro using the version just prior to Final Cut Pro X (a). A similar screen layout in Final Cut Pro X. It has the same essential layout as the older version, but with several key interface changes (b).

The central explanation for Apple's complete redesign of Final Cut begins with recognizing that the underlying technology was more than a decade old. Final Cut's release in 1999 came before Apple migrated to the current OS X operating system and Intel microprocessors, with 64-bit architecture allowing software to use more than 4 gigabytes of memory. All this new, high-performance technology was vital for video editing, during which the computer read, processed, and stored billions of bits of video information per second.

And with a giant leap in computer performance comes a giant leap in what software can offer the customer. Final Cut Pro X pushed the boundaries of what customers thought was possible. The Color Match feature could alter the color of video clips to reconcile different lighting, so one clip recorded at sunrise could match another recorded at high noon. The Find People and Smart Collections features automatically detected how many people were in a clip—one person, two people, group shots—and put them in virtual folders for easy reference. The Retiming feature let you stretch a clip to play back slower, or shrink it to play faster. The software could automatically fix video problems such as camera shake, or audio problems such as too much background noise. In earlier versions, any operation that didn't happen in real time would lock up the entire program and make you wait until it was finished. Final Cut Pro X processed complex changes in the background so you could keep working. The cumulative effect of this video editing power could change an editor's experience.

The Experience

Although editors appreciated the power of the new software, experienced professionals who could work quickly on the old, familiar Final Cut had to relearn the new program from scratch. The significant changes made to the video timeline, to take one major example, illustrate the challenges these professionals faced.

One of the main views in video editing software is the timeline, a series of horizontal lanes where editors arrange audio and video clips in chronological order. Traditionally there are many small icons scattered around the timeline that control various functions. Apple removed almost all of them, integrating the functions in other ways, such as enabling clicking directly on the video clip. The result was a clean, modern appearance that placed focus on the media instead of the controls—but this was different from every major editing platform to come before it (Figure 8.13).

FIGURE 8.13a

The top of the timeline in Avid 6 (left), a competitor of Final Cut. The same region in Final Cut Pro X (right).

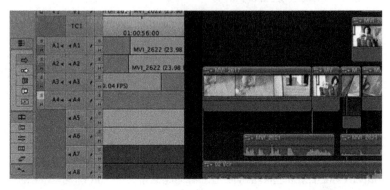

FIGURE 8.13b

The left edge of the timeline typically contains track numbers and other controls, as seen here in Avid 6 (left). Final Cut Pro X has none of these controls (right).

FIGURE 8.13c

The bottom of the timeline in Avid 6 (left) and in Final Cut Pro X (right).

Traditional editing software assigns a certain kind of media to each horizontal lane, called a "track," but Final Cut Pro X changed that, too. Michael Friedman, a producer and Emmy Award–winning editor whose credits include *The Amazing Race*, *Project Runway*, and *The Bachelor*, described his reaction:

> At first, editing without conventional timeline tracks felt unnerving. I did not like it. Like driving on a busy highway with no lane markers. As my first FCP X deadline approached, it was as if that unmarked highway was now rain-soaked and lit only by moonlight. It induced waves of panic. I typically

organize my audio tracks by content: natural sound on tracks 1 and 2; interviews on 3 and 4; music and FX on 5 through 8. When working with other editors, it makes it easier to collaborate with these standard track assignments.

In FCP X, that's gone. No track numbers. Just metadata. There are automated solutions for identifying music and dialogue, but the tracks are gone. . . . It's a departure from every major editing platform currently available. It's taken months to feel familiar, but the panic is now gone.

Similarly, traditional editing software like Avid 6 has modes for accessing various functions. For fine editing between shots, you click a button to enter Trim mode. Then you can trim the beginning and ending of clips but you can't perform other functions. Or if you want to add an effect like a wipe you go into Effect mode which is exclusively for manipulating effects. Final Cut Pro X does away with these modes. You can trim a clip or add an effect anytime.[8]

Technology-driven changes tend to happen periodically, but Apple's software interface changes were perhaps the most radical update to video editing in a decade. Friedman put this change in context:

Working in film and television for 20 years I'd personally seen editors unhappy with change many times before:

In 1995, I knew a flat-bed film editor who was resistant to non-linear editing and said "if I wanted to work on a computer, I'd be an accountant!" In the years that followed, he worked less and less.

When Final Cut Pro came along, I trained many seasoned Avid editors how to use the new software. More than a few said it was "not suitable for professional use." But in 2001, my first primetime television editing job was on Final Cut and, as recently as 2011, I edited *Project Runway* on FCP.

When FCP X came along, the grumpy and resistant editor was . . . me. While the new approach and interface intrigued me, I felt totally disoriented and was unable to perform even the most basic editing tasks. Mind you, I beta-tested version 1.0 of Final Cut in 1999 and loved it. Since then, I have spent more than 20,000 hours editing, mostly on Avid, but with healthy doses of FCP and Premiere as well.

In the 90s, I was an aspiring editor, but now I am a grizzled veteran. So, with version X, I said, "Why should I bother to learn yet another interface? Where's my FCP 8? What can X do that I can't do now? What's in it for me?"

However, having witnessed the waves of resistance to change in the past, thinking, "I may be missing the next big thing," I've forced myself to work through the discomfort and learn Final Cut Pro X.[9]

Friedman's experience was probably typical of the kind of explicit acceptance required of video editors to learn the new Final Cut. What he learned about the new software was that "instead of driving a car, it feels more like skiing or surfing. . . . When you get over the frustration, there is something fast, fluid and flexible in FCP X that I haven't experienced before."[10]

Of the customers who were unwilling to devote effort to relearning the software, why didn't they simply continue to use their existing software? I heard a few reasons. One was that they *liked* upgrading because they wanted the new features. Customers didn't feel they should have to give up what they already had to get the new functions. Another reason was that they felt they *should* upgrade. Apple, like most software companies, only supports older hardware and software for so long, and therefore many people try to ensure everything will work properly by keeping the hardware and software up to date. Yet another reason was that they *had to* upgrade: they were purchasing additional copies for their business and Apple had removed the old version of Final Cut from the App Store.

Reactions

The changes enraged customers to such a degree that the backlash became a public relations problem for Apple. David Pogue, a technology writer for the *New York Times*, wrote, "In 10 years of writing *Times* columns, I've never encountered anything quite like this. . . . After one day of using it, many professional video editors are running through the streets with pitchforks."[11] Mark Raudonis, head of postproduction at Bunim/Murray Productions said, "There has been more noise generated by this event than anything I can recall in my career. It was passionate, vocal, and persistent."[12] Richard Harrington, an industry veteran, wrote that trying to use the new version using workarounds to accomplish everyday tasks was like "telling a NASCAR driver to turn over their car, strap one roller skate on, and push as fast as possible with the other foot."[13] The Motley Fool, a financial investment website, published a series on what happened titled "Last Call for Final Cut?" Paul Skidmore, an independent filmmaker, summed up much of the criticism when he wrote, "This has alienated a lot of users—users like me that see Final Cut as the operating system for their business."[14]

One editor I spoke with said his reaction wasn't just about having to relearn the software. He said the power and ease of use of Final Cut Pro X was gradually enabling other people who weren't trained as editors, such as a director, to manipulate video as well as he did. He believed that eventually the software would make his skills obsolete.

Evolution

Some people in the industry and the media theorized that Apple cared less about serving the professional video market and more about the potentially much larger prosumer market of sophisticated nonprofessionals who edit video as a hobby and invest significant money and time in their tools. One clue to this strategy is that the price of Final Cut was slashed from $1,000 to $300. Whether or not this was Apple's intention, the company acted swiftly to repair the damage to its reputation among video professionals. Apple made the previous version of Final Cut available for sale to customers who couldn't work without the missing features. And in a surprising move for a company that rarely admits failure, product managers were sent out to meet with professional video editors to assure them that Apple would soon restore the missing features.

And restore missing features it did, releasing two rapid updates: one in mid-November 2011 and another (version 10.0.3) the following January. In addition, more third-party plug-ins were made available than for the previous version of Final Cut. Perhaps this was part of Apple's plan for easing customers' transition pains: working closely with plug-in software companies to help *them* make the transition to Final Cut Pro X.

The media largely recognized Apple's efforts. For example, *PC Magazine* named version 10.0.3 an Editor's Choice for high-end video editing software: "Thanks to both performance and ease-of-use features, pros may find that the same tasks take a fraction of the time they took in previous versions.... Final Cut Pro X is a delight to work in compared with other serious video editing software."[15]

Ironically, years before, Apple had taken the same approach to redesigning iMovie, its consumer video editing software, and received the same reaction from customers. For its part, Apple may have taken the public relations lesson to heart after the Final Cut debacle. While developing the Mountain Lion version of the Mac operating system, Apple gave journalists a copy even before the programmer community—a first.

Quantitative Results

It's hard to say how much actual customer disruption was caused by this redesign, and how much was just an expression of the initial shock. And it's also hard to know what the financial impact has been because Apple doesn't publicly release sales numbers.

Final Cut has two main competitors, both of whom had sales increases following the release of Final Cut Pro X: Adobe said sales of their Premier Pro video editing software rose 22 percent in three months, partially due to converting disgruntled Final Cut customers. Avid said that it had converted approximately 6,000 Final Cut customers to its software in six months.

But Final Cut Pro X survives and in fact has risen to become one of the highest-grossing apps in Apple's App Store. Customer ratings for the updated version 10.0.3 averaged 4.5 out of 5 stars, with comments such as:

- "Outstanding update."

- "Very easy and very powerful."

- "Bold move!"

- "Amazing."

Although some dissatisfied customers moved on, others found that Final Cut Pro X redeemed itself.

Lessons

The lesson in this chapter is about a trend that cuts across many industries: when technological advancements enable not only higher performance and new functions but also new and better experiences, embrace them, even if you face a short-term disruption. If you don't, inevitably a competitor will.

More specifically, the change has to start soon enough and go fast enough to compete. Nokia did change to embrace touchscreen technology, just not soon enough and fast enough. Here's the perspective of Matt Jones, a designer who worked at Nokia, in 2007:

> In recent months we've seen Nokia and Sony Ericsson show demos of their touch UIs [user interfaces]. To which the response on many tech blogs has been "It's a copy of the iPhone." In fact, even a Nokia executive responded that they had "copied with pride."
>
> That last remark made me spit with anger—and I almost posted something very intemperate as a result. The work that all the teams within Nokia had put into developing touch UI got discounted, just like that, with a half-thought-through response in a press conference. I wish that huge software engineering outfits like S60 could move fast enough to "copy with pride."
>
> Sheesh.
>
> Fact-of-the-matter is if you have roughly the same component pipeline, and you're designing an interface used on-the-go by (human) fingers, you're going to end up with a lot of the same UI principles.
>
> But Apple executed first, and beautifully, and they win.[16]

Symbian wasn't alone; Palm's WebOS and the BlackBerry suffered similar fates.

Looking back further in time, it's not hard to find more examples of this phenomenon. WordPerfect dominated the word-processing market during the 1980s when all PCs ran the DOS operating system. When the Macintosh arrived in 1984 and Windows in 1985, WordPerfect failed to comprehend the massive shift in human–computer interaction that was happening. WordPerfect moved slowly and fumbled the shift from DOS to Windows. Its entry into the market was two years later than the competition, and the new program was difficult to install, and buggy. Microsoft Word, which had trailed WordPerfect in market share for more than seven years, pounced on the weakened competitor and captured 94 percent of the market.

Redesign versus Gradual Change

Conversely, if you don't face a shift to a new enabling technology, drastic redesign may not be justified. Amazon is a good example of this: for more than 10 years Amazon has gradually updated its website design as the business evolved, always avoiding big redesigns. Simultaneously, the company has embraced new technologies by releasing new, device-appropriate designs for mobile phones, tablets, and the Kindle e-reader.[17]

Gerald Lohse and his colleagues conducted research on e-commerce website use over time, measuring the number of visits per person, length of sessions, and the timing and frequency of purchases.[18] They found that familiarity with a particular website makes visitors less likely to switch to a competitor's site because of the effort and time needed to become familiar with another site. They refer to this behavior as "cognitive lock-in." Essentially, people are creatures of habit.

If a site is redesigned, cognitive lock-in is lost, and customers must expend the same effort to relearn the site as to learn a competitor's site. Lohse found more cognitive lock-in at Amazon than at Barnes & Noble's site. A redesign has to offer enough of an experiential improvement to make up for the loss of cognitive lock-in.

A Better Experience

Customers may reject a redesign if they don't feel there is a clear benefit for them.[19] In 2011 Gawker rolled out a redesign of its news websites using unconventional navigation oriented around the type of content published rather than by how its visitors wanted to browse. Gawker subsequently faced a firestorm of criticism and lost viewers. The company rolled back the design a few weeks later.

And just because a new technology promises an interesting new experience doesn't necessarily mean it will be a *better* experience. For example, every few years someone touts a new 3D environment for accessing information on the Web powered by technologies such as VRML (virtual reality modeling language). These technologies look cool and always receive attention for their novelty and potential. But 3D on the Web has yet to find an application that offers people an experience worth returning to. Looking cool isn't enough.

Sometimes you won't know if a new design benefits customers until you try it. These cases are best treated as experiments, rolled out gradually and killed when they don't work. When Google launched Wave, a new kind of real-time messaging platform (see Chapter 2), the company started with a "preview" of what was coming and then launched a beta version to a limited audience. Even when launched publicly, Wave was categorized as part of the Google Labs collection of experimental apps. The product was too radical for most people and Google discontinued it after less than a year. Although most people were surprised that Google killed the product so quickly, there was no Final Cut Pro X level of anger because customers understood Wave was an experiment.

Every product has flaws. But customers will overlook flaws if their overall experience is good enough. Apple succeeds despite missing features because its products are (in its own words) magical. In less metaphorical terms, Apple pushes the limits of industrial design and software design to achieve unexpectedly high usability and aesthetics. The iPhone was long criticized for lacking features other smartphones had, such as multitasking, but the experience of using the iPhone is so delightful that customers generally overlook the omissions. Final Cut Pro X flubbed the initial feature list, but righted the ship quickly enough.

What can look like failure in the short term for Apple is actually part of a successful long-term approach. If we look back at the history of Apple's product portfolio, we can see a pattern in its major design changes, such as the 1994 transition from Macintosh 68000 to PowerPC microprocessors, or the 2011 transition from MobileMe to iCloud. There are three major steps to these transitions:

1. Proactively discontinue technology that's a strategic dead end, even if the technology is popular and there is a large installed base of products.

2. Launch new technology with slick, forward-looking design, even if the product is incomplete.

3. Dedicate the next few product versions to reinstating the missing features.

Apple moves quickly to avoid stagnation. Though Apple-style change scares other companies, the risk of not changing is obsolescence. Apple's customers have to cope with frequent change, but that's less disruptive than the disappearance of an entire platform or company.

Summary

Symbian

What it is: Symbian is a mobile phone operating system. A coalition of companies devoted more than 13 years to developing and designing it. Nokia alone has sold more than 385 million Symbian-powered phones.

Why the experience failed: The first Symbian touchscreen phones, introduced in 2008, had software usability and performance problems. By the time Nokia released robust touchscreen devices and software in 2010, competitors had surpassed Nokia both in product design and market share.

The underlying cause: Touchscreens imposed a change on the interaction paradigm, offering new, more interesting experiences. Nokia timidly entered this world with old hardware technology and half-baked software, in part to retain backward compatibility with the established Symbian platform. The makers of the iPhone and Android phones started fresh with the latest hardware and new software to realize the full potential of the touchscreen experience.

The lesson: When there's a technological shift from quantitative performance improvements to qualitative product design, a corresponding shift must be made in how the product is conceived and constructed.

Final Cut Pro X

What it is: Final Cut is Apple's video editing software intended mainly for video professionals. The product has been developed over the course of more than 13 years and is used by approximately two million people. Final Cut Pro X was a ground-up redesign to take advantage of contemporary hardware that enabled it to offer amazing new features.

Why the experience failed: Customers, often feeling obliged to update to the latest version, faced a software interface radically different than previous versions and from industry standards. The software also lacked key features that editors needed to do their work. Apple reinstated these missing features within six months, satisfying those who were willing to learn the new interface design to benefit from Final Cut's new capabilities.

The underlying cause: Apple apparently misjudged how much current customers relied on certain features, and alienated them by not testing Final Cut Pro X with them before the public release. Apple then made the situation worse by pulling the previous version off the market.

The lesson: When technological advancements enable not only higher performance and new functions but also new and better experiences, embrace them. You don't have to lose current customers in the process: include them in product planning and provide a smooth path to every upgrade.

CHAPTER 9

Why We Fail

> Vulnerability is our most accurate measurement of courage.
>
> —Brené Brown, authentic leadership researcher,
> University of Houston

Experience Matters

Late in 2010 a technologist who worked at Symbian for several years published his explanation for why Symbian failed.[1] Upon reading it, science fiction author and futurist Bruce Sterling had this to say.

> Sometimes I think that EVERY dead medium dies like this—for reasons that may seem easy for pundits to explain in retrospect—"the iPhone appeared"—but are, in reality, incredibly complicated, satanically detailed and paralyzingly boring to all outsiders.
>
> I bet if you went over to AOL and Yahoo! right now and asked people in the know: "You guys had it all once! Where did it go?" you'd get a twenty-volume, bag-of-tangled-yarn exegesis. And I wish I could tell you that this story would be really fascinating. But it isn't. I mean, try reading this Symbian guy's explanation, if you can.
>
> About the only way to make a slow-motion train wreck of this kind seem fascinating is to personalize it and blame it on particular bad guys, but although this always compels some public attention, it's basically demagoguery. Explaining why Symbian failed is like explaining why it rained last Wednesday. There were some physical reasons why it rained, but if you ran the tape of dead-media explanation back, you would find it was all contingent.[2]

I tend to think Sterling is right. My telling of the Symbian story in Chapter 8 doesn't entirely explain "why Symbian failed"; that tale would be almost as boring for you to read as it would be for me to write. So instead of relating the dysfunctional relationships in the Symbian Foundation, the mind-numbing difficulty of developing software for Symbian, and the inexplicable management infighting, I chose to write a more superficial but enjoyable story.

In all seriousness, I don't believe an exegesis on Symbian would necessarily help you avoid failure. Symbian's successors have made the same organizational mistakes and succeeded in spite of them. Google's relationship with its Android partners isn't all sweetness and light. Developing applications for the iPhone can be expensive and infuriating enough to put a small developer out of business. And yet Google and Apple overcome these problems because customers love the final result. If customers enjoy their experience and pay for it, then organizational faults are tolerated.

Throughout this book I've argued that the success of innovative digital products and services in the 21st century hinges less on objective design factors than it does on customers' subjective experiences. To avoid failure, avoid bad experiences.

That's easier said than done, of course. I've worked in technology design since 1994 and I think we still have only rudimentary tools for understanding our customers' expectations, desires, and emotions. The tools we have should be employed more often, and the results need to be recorded and analyzed so that the organization learns and the product improves.

Three Key Elements

The experience design profession has existed a short time compared with other fields and we would be wise to ask what others know about failure. Kathryn Schulz's book *Being Wrong* is a penetrating and philosophical treatise on failure in general. In it she examines industries and organizations that have suffered massive failures but learned to raise and control their quality. Aviation is one example. In 1938 when the U.S. Federal Aviation Administration starting tracking accidents, there were more than 125 accidents per 100,000 flight hours. That number has steadily declined and is now regularly under seven.[3] This record of improving safety results from examining how errors occur and using that knowledge to improve everything from the design of aircraft to the way pilots communicate.

In manufacturing, failure is now commonly avoided through quality control methods such as Six Sigma, a methodology that aims to measure the defects in a process and then systematically eliminate them. Six Sigma helped Motorola save $17 billion in defect-related costs between 1986 and 2006, all while improving product quality.

The methods used for quality control in aviation, manufacturing, and other industries appear vastly different, but Schulz found three elements that all quality control methods have in common:

1. Accept that errors happen.

2. Share information openly.

3. Gather verifiable data to correct errors.[4]

Accepting that small-scale errors happen is the first step in avoiding failure. If you don't accept that errors happen, you can't and won't do anything to fix them. Once you've accepted that errors happen, sharing that information openly helps your entire organization learn from the experience. And to truly understand the error, you need to measure it and produce verifiable data on which to act. Otherwise, you are relying on fallible opinions about what happened. Once you have verifiable data, you can work on how to avoid it next time.

These three elements—accepting errors, sharing information, and gathering data—sound obvious and self-evident. So why don't they happen all the time?

Accept That Errors Happen

After writing the case studies in this book, I reviewed them to look for patterns in the underlying causes of failure. There's a clear pattern of ignorance and/or denial in many of these situations, a pattern contrary to the accepting-sharing-gathering elements of quality control methods. For example:

- BMW erected a wall of public relations denial while hoping a flawed concept could redeem itself.

- The Google Wave team ignored the need to test with customers for far too long and then wouldn't admit there were fundamental problems with the design.

- The OpenID team acknowledged usability problems, but not to the extent necessary to fix design flaws until it was too late.

- Microsoft's decision to offer the Zune was a reasonable strategic move, but its release was executed without the market knowledge that would have sufficiently illuminated the dominance of their competition.

- Pownce denied that its service was similar to Twitter and subsequently failed to compete.

- Classmates.com settled lawsuits out of court rather than admit wrongdoing.

- Nokia thought incremental improvements were sufficient when threatened by competitors, but Apple and Google offered what everyone else understood were revolutionary designs.

- Apple's Final Cut Pro X rollout repeated the pattern of a crippled iMovie release years earlier, causing the same uproar from customers.

Denial of our faults is a well-known human characteristic leading to failure. Our egos and salaries depend on us being experts, so it's understandable when we shirk responsibility for screwups. But these were all sophisticated companies staffed by smart people, and in my experience there are usually deeper, subtler actions at work.

The actions of corporations are the actions of individuals made large. Like everyone else, designers are vulnerable to psychological phenomena that keep us from recognizing problems and doing something about them. But if we can learn to recognize a few of the most damaging biases, we can steer ourselves away from a lot of trouble.[5]

Sometimes we don't see what we don't want to see, a bias called *motivated blindness.* At work we're commonly motivated by money and other factors to get things done, not by a focus on problems. Those in charge at Plaxo chose to focus on their innovative business model and growth rate rather than the increasingly worrisome customer service complaints.

When we do see a problem, even a bad one, we're less likely to do something to fix it if other people also see the problem. This is called the *bystander effect.* Sometimes this happens because we assume someone else will fix it. Sometimes it is due to *pluralistic ignorance,* which is when we assume nothing is wrong because nobody else seems concerned. I have to wonder if the early OpenID Foundation directors had concerns about usability but didn't voice them strongly enough because other directors didn't.

Once we're in the middle of an uncomfortable problem, we sometimes use a coping mechanism called *normalcy bias* to convince ourselves everything is normal. Pretending that things are fine can feel better than acknowledging an ugly problem. This is what I heard when BMW Corporate Communications talked about iDrive.

Sometimes we have doubts about the ethicality or legality of our work but don't object because the situation is ambiguous and we fear we might be mistaken about whether there's actually a problem. I wouldn't be surprised if people working at Classmates.com felt this. I know I've struggled with ambiguous ethical problems in my work.

And sometimes we're not confident enough to do something because we have less experience, we're paid less, or we're in the minority.

Share Information Openly

You may think the above psychological biases are minor and don't actually lead to large-scale failure. After all, in corporate situations these biases are rarely investigated and reported. But it's not hard to find examples of major problems caused when biases cut off the flow of vital information.

In late 2009 there was a crisis of confidence in the financial world regarding Greece's ability to pay its debts. One thing led to another and by the following May the eurozone countries and the International Monetary Fund (IMF) agreed to loan Greece €110 billion to bail out the country.

How could this happen when there are clear rules that govern how eurozone countries run their economies to avoid this sort of failure? When Greece was applying to enter the eurozone, the Greek Ministry of Finance fabricated the economic numbers to make a fair situation look good. The eurozone authorities knew the numbers were fabricated, but in a case of motivated blindness, they said nothing. Here's one economist's explanation:

> In just a few years, Greece seemed to get its house in order. The country made unbelievable strides in its financial data to meet the [eurozone] criteria. Truly unbelievable. Did anybody believe them?
>
> "No," says Jacob Kirkegaard with the Peterson Institute for International Economics.
>
> But the euro was supposed to be about unity. Countries were saying we are mature, civilized European nations with strong financials. Kirkegaard says no one wanted to stand up and say to Greece—"you are lying." Also, Kirkegaard says there were a lot of comparisons to Sweden popping up in those meeting rooms—as in, we're all Swedes now.
>
> "When that is the self-identity, all of a sudden standing up and saying to one member of this club that look, actually, you're dirty, well they're going to turn around and say what about yourself?" says Kirkegaard. "You know, who is to say if you can't trust the Greeks can you really trust the Italians?"
>
> Because, really, once you asked that question, the answer was likely to be no.[6]

That sort of irresponsibility cost Greeks hundreds of thousands of jobs and their quality of life, as well as causing economic stress on the other 16 eurozone countries.

Sometimes silence in the face of danger costs more than money. In February 2011 a group of 16 skiers convened for a trip down Cowboy Mountain near Seattle. The group was a who's who of experienced skiers in the area, people such as Elyse Saugstad, a professional freeskier; John Stifter, editor of *Powder* magazine; Megan Michelson, a freeskiing editor at ESPN.com; Erin Dessert and Tim Wangen, both locals with decades of experience on the mountain; and Jim Jack, head judge of the Freeskiing World Tour. The group also included local experts who had skied the mountain many times. They carried safety gear. And they had read the avalanche report that told them there was a considerable chance of snow sliding that day.

As they neared the top of the mountain, at least a few of them had concerns about their safety. But as various biases surfaced in their minds, no one said anything.

> "If it was up to me, I would never have gone backcountry skiing with [more than] 12 people," Michelson, the ESPN journalist, said. "That's just way too many. But there were sort of the social dynamics of that—where I didn't want to be the one to say, you know, 'Hey, this is too big a group and we shouldn't be doing this.' I was invited by someone else, so I didn't want to stand up and cause a fuss. And not to play the gender card, but there were 2 girls and 10 guys, and I didn't want to be the whiny female figure, you know? So I just followed along."

> "I've been riding Stevens Pass since I was 3 years old," Dessert said. "I can tell circumstances, and I just felt like something besides myself was in charge. They're all so professional and intelligent and driven and powerful and riding with athletic prowess, yet everything in my mind was going off, wanting to tell them to stop."

> "I could see the others when I cut over," Wangen said. "I thought: Oh yeah, that's a bad place to be. That's a bad place to be with that many people. But I didn't say anything. I didn't want to be the jerk."

> Elyse Saugstad, a professional skier, wore a backpack equipped with an air bag, a relatively new and expensive

part of the arsenal that backcountry users increasingly carry to ease their minds and increase survival odds in case of an avalanche. About to be overtaken, she pulled a cord near her chest. She was knocked down before she knew if the canister of compressed air inflated winged pillows behind her head. . . .

At first she thought she would be embarrassed that she had deployed her air bag, that the other expert skiers she was with, more than a dozen of them, would have a good laugh at her panicked overreaction. Seconds later, tumbling uncontrollably inside a ribbon of speeding snow, she was sure this was how she was going to die.[7]

Thirty minutes after they started skiing, three of them were dead. Elyse Saugstad, who acted despite her fear of embarrassment, survived.

One of the best ways to avoid failure is to say something. Out loud. We might be the least experienced person around a conference room table full of experts, and we might be afraid, but chances are if the concern is warranted, other people will have it too. And managers need to be open to this kind of transparent communication in order to avoid failed projects.

I was reminded of this recently when a friend told me a story about a company he had advised in the late 1990s. The company wanted to create an online service that would allow people to select their favorite songs and then buy a custom-made CD of those songs, which would be sent to them in the mail. The company was essentially reinventing the "mix tapes" people used to create with cassettes. Because this was during the early days of mp3 audio files, my friend knew everyone would soon have the ability to create their own custom CDs right on their computers; they wouldn't need to pay a service and then wait for a CD to arrive in the mail. But the company didn't want him to question whether the customer experience would be a good one or not; they just wanted him to try to make them a success. He did try. But they weren't.

Scott Berkun, who served as a program manager at Microsoft for nine years, thinks that this sort of denial is "Microsoft's greatest disease":

The greatest disease at Microsoft is lack of sharing lessons from failure, especially where innovation is concerned. Microsoft has made many big, visible bets. Many of them have failed, but that's par for the course. The problem is these expensive lessons are swept under the rug, encouraging others in the company to repeat the same mistakes. Everyone loves to make fun of Microsoft Bob, but few can articulate why it failed. If you don't understand why it failed, you don't have any reason for laughing so hard, and you likely aren't half as smart as you think you are. A case study on Vista, MSN Search, Microsoft Bob, The Tablet PC, etc. should be produced by an outside consultant, and stapled on the forehead of every manager at the company, once a day, until they read them all word for word. Then they'd take advantage of Microsoft's so called experience and wisdom. Otherwise, they are being set up to make the same expensive mistakes again and again.[8]

Use Verifiable Data to Correct Errors

Identifying and gathering objective data is easy in fields such as online sales or in cases where qualitative testing can meet some easily understood threshold such as "at least 75 percent of our current customers can update their software in 10 minutes or less." Among the cases in this book, OpenID, BMW iDrive, Google Wave, and Symbian lacked simple but essential usability data to reveal to their creators the scale of the problems. Getting usability right isn't the only key to success, but it would have been a big step in the right direction.

These failures went beyond mere usability, however. Ideally designers would measure customers' experience with a new product, though this is harder. As covered in Chapter 1, contemporary digital products and services are complex, people's reasons for using them are multifaceted, and their experiences of them are emotional and subjective. Even when testing is conducted, it's usually about only one facet of the product, such as usability, and the testing measures only a short time span of the customer's experience. So it's not surprising when product teams lack an understanding of what their customers are experiencing.

Final Cut Pro X, the Zune, and Pownce needed more than an assessment of usability. Final Cut changed both its feature set and its interface, so Apple could have benefited from understanding which features were vital but also how customers perceived the learning curve. Pownce needed to know if groups of people would use the service on an ongoing basis instead of, or in addition to, other social media services. Microsoft needed to know if the Zune was more attractive than the iPod to some segment of the market based on their points of differentiation.

Thread the Line

Timidity does not beget innovation. As designers, if we are to accept the risk inherent in creating something new, we must be passionate in our position, and we must believe strongly that our way is the right way. It is this utmost confidence that leads companies such as BMW to consistently produce excellent products and confidently proclaim that their product is the "ultimate driving machine."

But to accept errors and share information about our faults with others requires humility. Our challenge then is to simultaneously hold two seemingly contradictory positions in our minds: the utter confidence in ourselves to overcome obstacles and the vulnerability to understand how we have erred and must change. It requires being passionate about a vision while being willing to change a product or strategy to achieve that vision.

For some this amounts to cognitive dissonance—like admitting the ultimate driving machine might contain a fundamental flaw.

Joe Kraus, an investing partner at the Google Ventures venture capital fund, puts it this way:

> In my mind, the ones who have no fear of failure are merely the dreamers, and the dreamers don't build great companies. The people that thread the line between vision and being able to execute and having this healthy fear of failing that drives them— not paralyzes them, but drives them—to be more persistent, to work harder than the next person, that's a magic formula.[9]

Rock 'n' roll legend Bruce Springsteen gave similar advice to young musicians:

> Rumble, young musicians, rumble. Open your ears and open your hearts. Don't take yourself too seriously, and take yourself as seriously as death itself. Don't worry. Worry your ass off. Have unclad confidence, but doubt. It keeps you awake and alert. Believe you are the baddest ass in town—and you suck! It keeps you honest. Be able to keep two completely contradictory ideals alive and well inside of your heart and head at all times. If it doesn't drive you crazy, it will make you strong. And stay hard, stay hungry and stay alive. And when you walk on stage tonight to bring the noise, treat it like it's all we have—and then remember it's only rock 'n' roll.[10]

CHAPTER 10

Avoid Failure

> Truth—more precisely, an accurate understanding of reality—
> is the essential foundation for producing good outcomes.
>
> —Ray Dalio, founder of the American investment
> management firm Bridgewater Associates,
> which he started as a one-person company and
> grew into the world's largest hedge fund company
> with $122 billion in assets under management

Although there is no secret formula for creating successful customer experiences, what I can offer you is a method to help you avoid failure while you search for successful designs. These recommendations counter the deficiencies identified in the previous chapter and throughout this book, namely:

- We're all vulnerable to psychological biases that make it difficult to accept errors and share information about problems.

- Contemporary digital products and services engage us in more complex ways, and because our reasons for using them are multifaceted, our experiences of them are emotional and subjective. They are *experiential products*, so testing product performance alone is insufficient to avoid failure.

A Method That Avoids Failure

Our method helps us avoid failure in several ways:

- It helps us build an accurate understanding of reality by generating verifiable data.

- It can be adopted by an entire organization because it reflects the needs of design, technology, and management.

- It allows us to research and test the customers' experience, not just the product or service.

- It covers everything from customers' perceptions of brand and design to the ability to use and interact with a product.

- It uses a realistic amount of resources to get the job done.

An Accurate Understanding of Reality

In experience design and other fields, there is an abundance of methodologies for innovation and controlling quality. Several of the methodologies that thrive today share a common thread that can help us measure customer experiences—the same essential method that has contributed to hundreds of years of scientific progress: the *scientific method*.

This is the same scientific method that we learned about in school, and it can be summarized in four steps:

1. Make an observation.

2. Form a hypothesis.

3. Run an experiment.

4. Interpret the results.

Let's say a chemist makes an educated guess that mixing two chemicals will produce a new chemical that has the properties she's looking for. She doesn't merely think about what *should* work, write down the formula, and send it to the manufacturing team. She mixes the chemicals and then measures what happens. The results may not be quite right but they may be close, and they help her make another guess that leads to another experiment. Gradually she creates what she's looking for. This deliberate, iterative method underlies our civilization's massive scientific progress since the 17th century. Only through first-hand observation do we have an accurate understanding of reality.

Depending on your perspective, the need for this kind of rigor may sound obvious, especially if you're already doing something like this on a departmental level, such as online marketing. Or it may sound too scientific, if for example, your practice follows an auteur model where designs emanate from someone's creative vision alone. Ultimately, design is about creating something that works for people, and we can use a methodical process for discovering if that something did indeed work.

The initial decades of digital design were about understanding new technology and acclimating to new product and service paradigms. There was a long learning curve and a lot of failure, mine included. Now we're acclimated to the technology, and we're ready to be more methodological about how we conceptualize, design, and test our ideas.

In design, software development, and business management—as in science—the scientific method holds the key to discarding years of amateurish guessing about what will succeed and replacing it with a way of discovering what we need to know by testing the viability of anything that is new and uncertain. The story of how each of these disciplines adopted and adapted the scientific method can help us apply it to our work.

Scientific Methods

The Scientific Method and Design

Since the 1960s, computers have had interfaces for humans to interact with them, but it wasn't until the 1980s that there were widespread efforts to ensure these interfaces were easy to use.[1] When the entire design revolved around what the person using the computer wanted and needed, the approach was called *user-centered design* (Figure 10.1). This philosophy formed the foundation of the fields of ergonomics and human factors, and—with the explosive growth of the Internet—disciplines such as user experience design, interaction design, and information architecture.

FIGURE 10.1
User-centered design
is an iterative cycle
starting with research
to understand how
people will use the
system. Designs are
documented and pro-
totypes are made and
tested with customers.
Test results contribute
to the research.

If you're familiar with techniques associated with user-centered design, you might be thinking, "We already research customers, make prototypes, and test them with customers. We've been doing this for decades!" That's true, and yet many of the products profiled in this book employed user-centered design techniques in one form or another. These techniques are effective and important, but they're not sufficient to achieve a great customer experience in the marketplace.

One shortcoming of user-centered design is that it isn't a method; it's a philosophy and a collection of techniques. It's not a methodology a business adopts and follows in the same way a business would follow Six Sigma, for example. So user-centered design often becomes subsumed by software development methodologies such as Rational Unified Process or Extreme Programming—and becomes diluted in the process.

A related shortcoming is that user-centered design and its offshoots exist at the team level of an organization. Teams have to appeal to business leaders to fully execute their work, and even when the design work is excellent, it exists somewhere inside a larger business process that ultimately determines the customer experience. For example, I know designers who were at Nokia doing wonderful work, but much of it was filtered out by the engineering-centric culture before reaching the market. What's needed is user-centered design at the organizational level. And to work at that level, a method must provide a way to integrate user-centered design with business strategy and the means of production (e.g., software development).

The Scientific Method and Software Development

As far back as the 1950s, a portion of the software development community has felt dissatisfied with heavyweight, top-down, waterfall methods for planning software. Because the traditional methods push most of the customer testing to the end, failures weren't exposed until projects were almost complete, after enormous resource expenditure. By the mid-1990s, methods such as Scrum and Extreme Programming provided alternative ways of working that were more collaborative and iterative. This movement crystallized in 2001 when a group of influential developers wrote the Manifesto for Agile Software Development. The Manifesto accelerated the acceptance of this alternative view and lent the category name of "agile" to all of the collected methods that follow this philosophy. Agile techniques are now used in almost half of all software development.[2] The Manifesto is succinct and worth reproducing in its entirety:

> We are uncovering better ways of developing software by doing it and helping others do it. Through this work we have come to value:
>
> • Individuals and interactions over processes and tools
>
> • Working software over comprehensive documentation
>
> • Customer collaboration over contract negotiation
>
> • Responding to change over following a plan
>
> That is, while there is value in the items on the right, we value the items on the left more.[3]

The tenets of "customer collaboration" and "responding to change" echo the parallel steps of research and iteration in user-centered design (and in milestone planning and discovery-driven planning, described below).

Whereas the scientific method requires us to identify individual hypotheses and test them, agile software development breaks the work into smaller batches that can be individually created and tested (Figure 10.2). Some agile methods, such as Extreme Programming, even require writing the tests first, forcing us to make explicit hypotheses about what the software is supposed to achieve.

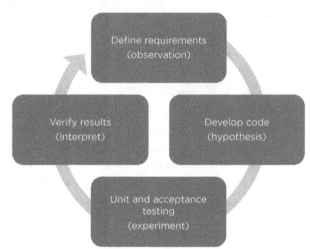

FIGURE 10.2
As in user-centered design, the essential stages of agile software development also reflect the stages of the scientific method.

Agile methods revolutionized how software is created, but they often lack a strong perspective on the customer experience. For example, "customer" in agile can mean the manager at the company who requested the software rather than an actual consumer who will buy and use the finished product.

The Scientific Method and Business Management

The work to apply the scientific method to business ventures extends back at least as far as the late 19th century and Frederick Winslow Taylor's Scientific Management, which has a point of view on manufacturing, management, and human factors. Some of Taylor's ideas can be found in the Toyota Production System (1948), which led directly to Lean Manufacturing (1988), which in turn influenced Lean Startup (2008), discussed below.

The use of the scientific method to explicitly plan new products and businesses dates back to 1985, when Zenas Block and Ian MacMillan proposed Milestone Planning, a method of testing hypotheses at certain milestones of a new venture:

Starting a new business is essentially an experiment. Implicit in the experiment are a number of hypotheses (commonly called assumptions) that can be tested only by experience. The entrepreneur launches the enterprise and works to establish it while simultaneously validating or invalidating the assumptions. Because some will be dead wrong and others partially wrong, an important goal of the business plan must be to continually produce and build on new knowledge. Managers must justify moving to each new stage or milestone in the plan on the basis of information learned in the previous stage.[4]

Block and MacMillan outline the significant milestones, such as "concept testing" and "prototype." Each milestone is associated with a number of hypotheses that must be tested. Whereas traditional milestones are associated with calendar dates, these milestones are only reached if the hypotheses are tested and iterated upon to find acceptable results. Block and MacMillan describe a number of tenets that are now becoming standard practice with technical entrepreneurs:

- Learning (i.e., "sharing information openly") becomes a key goal of testing hypotheses, "valuable not only for venture managers but also for investors, senior corporate managers, and directors."

- The learning enables "replanning" the venture while the venture is already under way, fueling a possible significant change in strategy, product design, or marketing. In current lingo we call this a *pivot*.

- Plans have milestones determined by tested hypotheses instead of the traditional predetermined dates. "The problem with date milestones is that they are totally unreliable for new ventures."

- Investing becomes less risky, because successive rounds of funding can be tied to each milestone, which are only reached if the hypotheses are proven true.

Block and MacMillan cite the example of 3M's introduction of the Thermofax, an early chemical-free photocopier. 3M's hypothesis was that researchers in libraries would be the perfect customers for the machine. The company experimented with offering the machines to researchers and found it wasn't a profitable market. But the testing helped them discover a demand for the machine in business offices and, after redesigning the machine and further testing, they found success by focusing on selling the machine to businesses.

Clayton Christensen's influential book *The Innovator's Dilemma* urges similar action for companies wanting to create disruptive innovations: "The risk is very high that any particular idea about the product attributes or market applications of a disruptive technology may not prove to be viable. Failure and iterative learning are, therefore, intrinsic to the search for success with a disruptive technology."[5] Christensen cites the work of Ian MacMillan and Rita Gunther McGrath, who continued the evolution of Milestone Planning with their 1995 publication "Discovery-Driven Planning."[6] They highlight the drawbacks of traditional planning tools, such as the financial models commonly used for predicting the performance of conventional lines of business. Financial models work when they allow people to make educated guesses based on past performance, but there is no past performance for new lines of business; a firm must run experiments to understand the potential costs and revenue at stake. Organizations such as the Salvation Army, DuPont, and Air Products report success using the discovery-driven planning technique.

Customer Development, a methodology published in 2005 by serial entrepreneur Steve Blank, offers practical steps for applying scientific method–based ideas for determining the strategy, marketing, and product development of a technology startup (Figure 10.3).[7] Like a scientist who carefully breaks a larger goal into smaller hypotheses he can test, Blank recommends building a minimum feature set into a product and then testing ideas with actual customers for realistic results. "In a startup no facts exist inside the building, only opinions."[8] Similar to Milestone Planning and Discovery-Driven Planning, Blank outlines four stages of growth any startup goes through. Within each stage, the testing of hypotheses drives the learning process. Here's how Eric Ries, creator of the Lean Startup methodology, described it:

> The nice thing about this paradigm is it sets the company up for a rational discussion when the task of finding customers fails. You can start to think through the consequences of this information before it's too late. You might still decide to press ahead building the original product, but you can do so with eyes open, knowing that it's going to be a tough, uphill battle. Or, you might start to iterate the concept, each time testing it against the set of facts that you've been collecting about potential customers. You don't have to wait to iterate until after the splashy high-burn launch.[9]

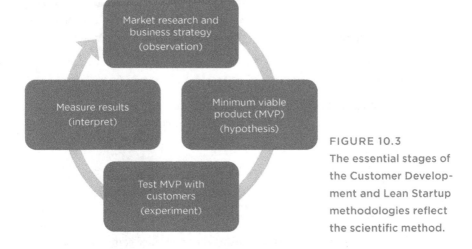

FIGURE 10.3
The essential stages of the Customer Development and Lean Startup methodologies reflect the scientific method.

The technology startup community drives much of the current demand and thinking in scientific method–based techniques because they must. Few industries assume so much risk and so much investment. They also drive this thinking because they *can*, having the ability to quickly prototype and test new business ideas. So it's among startups that Blank's Customer Development methodology and agile programming thrive. The next logical step was to use them together.

Lean Startup, a method developed by Eric Ries, combines the principles of Customer Development and agile programming and takes inspiration from Lean Manufacturing, a process developed in Japan during the second half of the 20th century. Lean Manufacturing is largely based on the Toyota Production System, which was designed to eliminate any work that doesn't produce value for customers, as opposed to trying to squeeze more value out of a factory. In staying lean, a startup can move quickly and inexpensively to validate more hypotheses and figure out what product fits which market before running out of money. Ries emphasizes using metrics that truly indicate a customer is receiving value, and evolved the idea of launching a minimal set of features with a Minimum Viable Product, similar to a prototype in user-centered design and a release in agile development. Several startups, such as Dropbox, IMVU, and Groupon, have reported success with this approach.[10]

These design, development, and management approaches all have something in common: they identify the part of the process that has the most uncertainty and target it with an iterative prototype-test-learn cycle.

As we've seen in the case studies in this book, experience failures can originate in any of these areas, so we can learn from all of these disciplines and add an iterative learning cycle where we have the most uncertainty.

The Experience Development Method

Standing on the shoulders of the scientific method–based approaches that came before, I developed a method called Experience Development (Figure 10.4). It includes the key characteristics of preceding methods, notably:

- Formulate testable hypotheses.
- Test the hypotheses with customers using prototypes.
- Plan with milestones instead of dates.
- Iterate on the above steps using the knowledge gained to establish experience, financial, and other metrics.

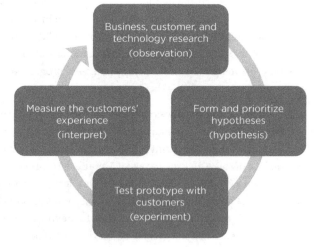

FIGURE 10.4
The essential stages of the Experience Development method.

The Experience Development method includes two key additions:

1. Hypotheses, prototypes, tests, and measurements are created by an integrated team of management, design, and development specialists.

2. Hypotheses and testing methods specifically address the customer experience.

Here's an overview of the basic steps of the method. For more detailed instruction on related methods see the resources listed at the end of this chapter.

Step 0: Organize around the Customer Experience

Before using the method, an organization should assemble a small, integrated team that works in time spans corresponding to the problems at hand. To begin, first determine if the relevant hypotheses are strategic (long-term) or tactical (short-term).

Strategic hypotheses concern major new features, major changes, a new product, or even a new business in which the customer experience is critical to success in the long term. The hypotheses in Table 10.1 illustrate major product development issues. Work on strategic problems requires a dedicated team for an extended period to iteratively test and update hypotheses to refine the solution.

Tactical hypotheses concern small new features and small changes that affect short-term success. For example, "If we simplify this key screen by moving all the optional information to another screen, then 90 percent of customers will complete the form faster and report higher satisfaction." We may have hypotheses about whether the hardware is fast enough or whether the customer service chat is effective. The process for creating and testing more tactical hypotheses is the same. Unlike strategic hypotheses, tactical hypotheses may not require a dedicated team or continuous activity. They can be tested at set intervals, such as at the beginning of each six-week sprint in an agile process, or following quarterly competitive benchmark reviews.

A characteristic of this method is keeping tests small so that many iterations can be performed and more can be learned. This is accomplished more quickly by a team that is as small as possible. It's not surprising that Customer Development emerged from and thrives at startup companies, because they are usually small by nature. If your organization is small, you're set. If your organization is large, you may need to create a subgroup of specialists that can work autonomously to quickly move through the entire iterative cycle of prototyping, testing, and learning. The Skunk Works configuration pioneered by Lockheed and copied widely provides a model where innovative development can blossom even within large, complex, bureaucratic organizations. Here are some of the rules created by Kelly Johnson, who ran Lockheed's Skunk Works in the early years:

- The Skunk Works' program manager must be delegated practically complete control of his program in all aspects. He should report to a division president or higher.

- The number of people having any connection with the project must be restricted in an almost vicious manner. Use a small number of good people.

- A very simple drawing and drawing release system with great flexibility for making changes must be provided in order to make schedule recovery in the face of failures.

- There must be a minimum number of reports required, but important work must be recorded thoroughly.

- The contractor [Lockheed] must be delegated the authority to test his final product in flight. He can and must test it in the initial stages. If he doesn't, he rapidly loses his competency to design other vehicles.

- Access by outsiders to the project and its personnel must be strictly controlled.

- Because only a few people will be used in engineering and most other areas, ways must be provided to reward good performance by pay, not simply related to the number of personnel supervised.[11]

We've seen customer experience failures that emanate from various disciplines, not just design. So this method requires an integrated team of management, design, and development specialists working in concert, conceptualizing the strategic advantage and executing on a prototype and test that accurately proves or disproves the hypothesis. For example, a minimally small software team would include one person knowledgeable in strategy and marketing, another in design and research, and another in programming. When creating prototypes for testing, passing requirements "over the wall" to a design or development department or a vendor will result in suboptimal results.

In other methods, the responsibility for customer research can be delegated to anyone, but if product success relies on a positive customer experience, it's vital that an experienced professional performs the research. We shouldn't expect stellar research results from someone who has little research experience any more than we should expect a graphic designer to write quality software code.

Step 1: Understand the Customer Experience

Modern technology companies conduct research all the time. They scan competitors' patent applications, monitor technology pipelines, and benchmark performance. Companies whose success depends on experiential products also need to observe their customers' experiences. For example, they should be aware of what their new customers expect and how well those expectations are being met by the products. What emotions do the customers feel? How do they actually use the products? What are the expectations, emotions, and actions of the *competitors'* customers? And because these all change over time, the observations need to happen as regularly as internal performance reviews. Out of these observations come testable hypotheses.

Team members usually have ideas about what may go wrong, but are sometimes hesitant to share them. A pre-mortem is one way to elicit these ideas. A pre-mortem is the opposite of a post-mortem: at the beginning of a project, I pose the hypothetical that the project has failed. I then ask the team why they think it failed, and what changes would have helped avoid the failure. We can then turn those hypothetical solutions into testable hypotheses and test them.

I must emphasize that to avoid the failures outlined in this book, you need to observe the *experience*, not the product (for a further explanation on the difference between experience and product refer to Chapter 1). Here's an example from the automotive world: Subaru collaborated with Toyota to build an affordable sports car that would be wonderful to drive. The project team culled design ideas from what made past models enjoyable to drive and developed a prototype. During testing the engineers iteratively formed hypotheses about what would work better, made adjustments, ran tests, and measured the results. But although they were modifying the prototype car, it was not the car they measured:

> We didn't set up any numerical targets like lap times or acceleration. We had one test driver, and after each set of tests, the only thing we'd ask was, "did you enjoy it?"
>
> Of course he said "yes" every time. The most important thing for me was—well, we say it like this: you must have a smile behind the wheel.[12]

A smile is one of the better outward signs of a good experience. Although many of us may like our cars, how many of us have cars that make us smile when we drive them?

The result of all that smiling is the 2012 Subaru BRZ, also known as the Scion FR-S and the Toyota GT86, a $28,000 four-seat coupe. Though it's not as fast, flashy, or technologically interesting as other sports cars, it has been praised by customers and automotive journalists.

You can see this shift to measuring experience among automotive media as well. For example, the Winding Road automotive website has a ranking system called the Involvement Index that ranks cars according to how well they engage the driver rather than how fast they accelerate or how many gadgets they include.

Motor Trend magazine does something similar now, ranking the Best Driver's Cars each year. In the 2012 test, the Subaru BRZ placed fourth, beating an $84,000 Jaguar, a $295,000 McLaren, and even a $393,000 Lamborghini.

Step 2: Form a Hypothesis

As we observe, we come up with questions. What if we left out features x, y, and z to make the product faster? What if we wrote more humorous copy? What if we let people customize it more? Before we can test these questions, we turn them into hypotheses that make it clear what is being tested and what results we expect.

With my perfect hindsight I'll use as examples the products profiled in this book. For each product, I created a sample hypothesis and a corresponding test (Table 10.1). My purpose here is not to second-guess what these companies did, but rather to illustrate how the method can work.

If we could travel into the future and see how products fail and then come back to the present, we would always know what changes to make. Or if we had infinite resources we could test everything. Because we can't do either of these things, we make educated guesses about which hypotheses are the most important.

Product	Hypothesis	Test
Microsoft Zune	If we offer an appealing subscription service, then 50% of people will find the Zune more attractive than the iPod.	Loan the Zune and the iPod to a trial group of target customers. When the trial period ends, offer them one to keep. Do at least 50% choose the Zune?
BMW iDrive	If drivers like the extensive iDrive features and novel design concept, then 90% will prefer cars with iDrive and will tolerate the required learning curve and longer task completion times.	Work through dealerships to identify customers ready to buy a 7-series car. Loan them a car with the conventional system for a week and then a car with iDrive for a week. Give them a choice to buy either. Do at least 90% choose iDrive?
Apple Final Cut Pro X	If we offer greatly improved interface design and performance, then 90% of customers will happily buy it despite a new learning curve and having to wait for missing features.	Share a private beta version with important customers to use in their daily work. Give them a choice to continue to use it or revert to the previous version. Do at least 90% continue to use the new version?
Nokia Symbian S60	If we make touchscreen modifications to Symbian S60, then 75% of current customers will continue to buy our phones instead of our competitors' phones.	Identify existing Nokia customers who are ready for a new mobile phone and loan them both a Nokia and an iPhone or Android phone. Offer them one to keep. Do at least 75% choose the Nokia?
Plaxo	If we greatly increase the volume of update request e-mails, fewer than 20% of non-customers will complain.	Increase the volume of update request e-mails sent from a small subset of customer accounts. Enable the non-customer recipients to send a complaint from a link in the e-mails. Do fewer than 20% complain?
OpenID	If we take our design that was favored by a niche audience and extend it to a mainstream audience, then 90% will be able to complete their first registration and sign in within three minutes.	Conduct traditional task-based usability testing with the new target audience. Can 90% register and sign in within three minutes?
Pownce	If we add group features to microblogging, then we will be sufficiently different than Twitter so that within one month at least 30% of Twitter customers will use Pownce instead of or in addition to Twitter.	Seed groups of customers who already use Twitter with a beta version of Pownce. After one month do at least 30% use Pownce alone or both Pownce and Twitter?
Wesabe	If customers have a choice between automatically importing their data or a manual method, then at least 60% will choose the manual method for the control and security it affords.	Prototype a system with automatic data import by actually making it work with one popular financial institution. Test it with a control group for a period, and then offer them the chance to switch back. Do at least 60% switch back?

Uncovering implicit assumptions and determining which ones are critical is one of the most difficult and ill-defined parts of scientific method–based methodologies. Working backward from the failures profiled in this book, we can generate relevant hypotheses by asking these questions:

1. What does our design do differently than the currently existing successful designs?

    For example, the key difference might be the product concept (iDrive, Wave), the interaction (iDrive, Wave, OpenID, Final Cut Pro X, Plaxo, Symbian), the audience (OpenID, Pownce), or the features (Final Cut Pro X).

2. We believe we have a particular competitive advantage, and that our customers' experiences are somehow better or different with our product. Do customers actually experience this difference?

    This question, in my experience, isn't asked nearly enough in contemporary experience design practice, especially given how many failures are due to losing to competitors (Zune, Wesabe, Pownce, Symbian).

3. Do our customers' experiences rely on technology performing in a new or better way?

    For example, Symbian's touchscreen interface suffered from delays between the touch and the on-screen feedback. Another classic example is Apple's Newton MessagePad, which when first released featured handwriting recognition that often produced unintelligible results.

4. Where could our current customer experience improve?

    From your observation, testing, and customer feedback, you should have an idea of which part of the experience is not pleasant, where there are too many steps, what abilities are missing, and so on. These are the places that competitors will target, as we saw with Wesabe.

Ranking these hypotheses to determine which are most important and deserve testing can be done using criteria relevant to your business, such as:

*   Which hypotheses arose from the most customer feedback?

*   Which are most important to our strategy?

*   Which are most important to our brand?

*   Which rely on the effects of external market forces, such as a social network reaching critical mass?

Table 10.2 illustrates a ranking of fictional hypotheses for the Microsoft Zune with notes explaining the prioritization.

TABLE 10.2 AN EXAMPLE OF PRIORITIZING FICTIONAL HYPOTHESES

Rank	Hypothesis	Prioritization Note
1	If we offer an appealing music subscription service, then 50% of people will find the Zune more attractive than the iPod.	Attitudinal market research indicates many consumers will choose a media player that allows them to purchase music by subscription. We need to validate whether they will prefer the Zune based on this differentiation.
2	If we create the ability to listen to a music collection on the PC, Zune, or Xbox, customers will prefer this as a superior experience.	The Zune could strengthen our platform strategy if it reinforced buying and using Windows and Xbox.
3	If our Metro operating system interface design is of equal quality to the competition, then 30% of customers will prefer our design and buy our device.	Interface design is a major customer preference point, so we need to discover how customers experience Metro versus the competition.
4	If our industrial design is of equal quality to the competition, then 30% of customers will prefer our design and buy our device.	Past research showed that industrial design is important but not critical to the customer experience. We can compete on industrial design but we don't think we will win on this factor, so it's not a high priority.
5	If we include HD radio and our competition does not, then 10% of customers will prefer our device.	Research to date suggests the radio is only a nice-to-have feature; we don't foresee it significantly influencing the customer experience.

Step 3: Run an Experiment

Along the spectra of attitudinal to behavioral and quantitative to qualitative, there are myriad customer research methods we might use to test a hypothesis. What's important is that we test the experience, not the product. For example, design researchers have ways to gauge desirability by measuring the emotions people feel while using a product. One way is to observe them, as in the Subaru example. Another is to ask people to indicate how they felt by looking at pictures of facial expressions and selecting one.

Adherents of Customer Development and Lean Startup sometimes use a proxy for experience called currency. In this technique, the potential customer is shown a prototype and asked to "pay" for the eventual real product. The currency can be an actual cash payment, but it can also be a noncash transaction in another form, such as a letter of intent. Currency demonstrates a commitment on the part of the customer, and requesting currency after testing a prototype can be easier than gauging experience directly. For example, Microsoft could have let target customers try a pre-production version of the Zune and asked them for a cash deposit, perhaps with the promise of getting the product before anyone else upon its release.

Step 4: Interpret the Results

One beautiful aspect of the scientific method is that the test results are usually true or false. Assuming the hypothesis is well stated with a clear threshold of failure, and that the test is appropriate and executed properly, there's little to interpret.

Contrast this with, for example, a product usability test performed without using a hypothesis, which was and is common. A customer would be asked to perform a number of typical tasks using a product while a researcher measured variables such as the time needed for task completion, the number of errors made, and how the customer rated his or her satisfaction with the product. After the tests, the accumulated data might not paint a clear picture of success or failure, leaving the researcher to ask, "Did the customers complete the tasks fast enough? Did they make too many errors? Is their level of satisfaction high enough?"

The hard work of interpretation happens when the test result is false. Then the team must decide what to do in the next iteration. Make a small change to the design? Change the code or hardware to perform differently? Alter the business model and make corresponding changes to the prototype? Being able to quickly move from a false test result to another iteration is why starting with a small, integrated team is so important.

Experience Development Summary

1. Is the problem strategic? If so, establish a dedicated, integrated team of specialists to work on a continuous basis. If the problem is tactical, the team can work on an as-needed basis. If inside a large organization, follow a Skunk Works model to create a small sub-group capable of working quickly.

2. Build an understanding of the current customer experience through customer research and competitive research, and by tapping internal wisdom through tools such as pre-mortems.

3. Form and prioritize hypotheses, especially concerning how the product is different from existing successful designs, the strategic differentiation as the customer experiences it, the performance of new technology, and known existing deficiencies in the experience.

4. Test the critical hypotheses.

5. Use the test results, particularly the false results, to re-prioritize and re-form the hypotheses, and begin the process again.

Conclusion

The case studies in this book demonstrate that contemporary digital products and services engage us in qualitatively more complex ways than in the past. Our reasons for using them are multifaceted. Our experiences of them are emotional and subjective. They are *experiential products*, and to avoid failure we have to go beyond understanding product performance to understanding customers' experiences.

In some cases, the product shortcomings were no secret but were ignored by those in charge. We're all vulnerable to psychological biases that make it difficult to accept errors and share information about problems. Methodologies based on the scientific method can make it safe to test ideas and have some fail, and to base decisions on verifiable data. The Experience Development method employs teams that integrate management, design, and technology so that test data can be shared naturally, a hallmark of quality control processes.

We have not yet proven beyond a doubt that these methods significantly and consistently improve the customer experience. But the empirical evidence we have so far is compelling. In addition to the success stories mentioned above, a number of venture capitalists support these methods, which is telling because they have the most at stake in terms of direct financial impact. Fred Wilson, a venture capitalist and principal at Union Square Ventures, reported that "There is a very high correlation between the lean startup approach and the top performing companies in our two funds."[13] And Scott Anthony at the *Harvard Business Review* cited Steve Blank and Rita Gunther McGrath as two of the twelve people in business history "who have brought the greatest clarity to the field of innovation," alongside the likes of Thomas Edison and Joseph Schumpeter.[14]

The allure of methods to some people is anathema to others. As with any approach, an overreliance on methods can become reductionist. Methods are tools, not instruction books. The method alone does not ensure success and doesn't obviate the need for a team with acute thinking. A good scientist invents effective, relevant hypotheses that all contribute to some larger proof. The experiments must be valid tests. And the results must be interpreted intelligently and objectively. As venture capitalist Fred Wilson remarked, "Lean startup is a machine; garbage in will give you garbage out."[15]

Resources

Philosophy

Being Wrong: Adventures in the Margin of Error, by Kathryn Schulz (New York: Ecco, 2010)

Background

Artful Making: What Managers Need to Know about How Artists Work, by Rob Austin and Lee Devin (Upper Saddle River, NJ: Financial Times Prentice Hall, 2003)

The Experience Economy, by B. Joseph Pine II and James H. Gilmore (Boston: Harvard Business, 2011)

Business

Discovery-Driven Growth: A Breakthrough Process to Reduce Risk and Seize Opportunity, by Rita Gunther McGrath and Ian C. MacMillan (Boston: Harvard Business, 2009)

The Entrepreneur's Guide to Customer Development: A "Cheat Sheet" to The Four Steps to the Epiphany, by Brant Cooper and Patrick Vlaskovits (2010; www.custdev.com)

The Lean Startup: How Today's Entrepreneurs Use Continuous Innovation to Create Radically Successful Businesses, by Eric Ries (New York: Crown Business, 2011)

Research and Testing

Observing the User Experience: A Practitioner's Guide to User Research, 2nd ed., by Elizabeth Goodman, Mike Kuniavsky, and Andrea Moed (Waltham, MA: Morgan Kaufmann, 2012)

Prototyping: A Practitioner's Guide, by Todd Zaki Warfel (Brooklyn, NY: Rosenfeld Media, 2009)

Design

About Face 3: The Essentials of Interaction Design, by Alan Cooper, Robert Reimann, and David Cronin (Indianapolis: Wiley, 2007)

Experience Design 1.1, by Nathan Shedroff (San Francisco: Experience Design Books, 2009)

Development

The Art of Agile Development, by James Shore and Shane Warden (Sebastopol, CA: O'Reilly, 2008)

References

Chapter 1

1. M. G. Siegler, "The Death of the Spec," *TechCrunch*, November 14, 2011, http://techcrunch.com/2011/11/14/rip-spec/.
2. Mike Gikas, "Lab Tests: Why Consumer Reports Can't Recommend the iPhone 4," *Consumer Reports*, July 12, 2010, http://news.consumerreports.org/ electronics/2010/07/apple-iphone-4-antenna-issue-iphone4-problems-dropped-calls-lab-test-confirmed-problem-issues-signal-strength-att-network-gsm.html.
3. "Apple Reports Fourth Quarter Results," Apple, October 18, 2010, www.apple.com/ pr/library/2010/10/18Apple-Reports-Fourth-Quarter-Results.html.
4. Marco Arment, "Consumer Reports," *Marco.org*, November 8, 2011, www.marco. org/2011/11/08/consumer-reports-iphone-4s.
5. B. Joseph Pine II and James H. Gilmore, *The Experience Economy*, updated ed. (Boston: Harvard Business, 2011), 5. Both this book and Nathan Shedroff's *Experience Design 1.1* should be part of the canon for anyone working in the field.
6. Pine and Gilmore, *Experience Economy*, 1–2.
7. Ibid., 19–20.
8. Ibid., 20–21.
9. Stephanie Clifford, "Malls' New Pitch: Come for the Experience," *New York Times*, July 17, 2012, www.nytimes.com/2012/07/18/business/malls-take-on-the-internet-by-stressing-the-experience.html?pagewanted=all&_r=1&.
10. Nathan Shedroff, *Experience Design 1.1* (San Francisco: Experience Design Books, 2009), 2.
11. A fascinating facet to this story is how a core technology underlying digital music players also favors experience over specs. For a long time the digital audio industry strived to accurately encode sound waves in a digital format. This required a lot of storage space for large digital files that represented all the sound in the music. MP3 files on the other hand record only *what we hear*, not all the sound in the air. Because the human ear doesn't hear everything, the resulting digital files can be much smaller. This innovation is called perceptual coding. You can read more about how it works in a paper I wrote here: www.noisebetweenstations.com/personal/essays/audio_on_the_internet/ MaskingPaper.html.
12. Darren Murph, "Microsoft Surface Tablets: The Differences between Windows RT and Windows 8 Pro Models," *Engadget*, June 18, 2012, http://engadget.com /2012/06/18/microsoft-surface-tablets-the-differences-between-rt-and-window/.

Chapter 2

1. Bill Buxton, *Sketching User Experiences: Getting the Design Right and the Right Design* (Burlington, MA: Morgan Kaufmann, 2007).
2. Maryam Tohidi et al., "Getting the Right Design and the Design Right: Testing Many Is Better Than One," April 22–27, 2006, www.billbuxton.com/rightDesign.pdf.
3. Oldsmobile, not Ford? Yes. But Ford is credited with taking mass production further by using assembly lines.
4. "Raining Luxury," *Automobile*, April 2009, www.automobilemag.com/ features/0309_luxury/.
5. *Top Gear*, Season 1, Episode 5, British Broadcasting Corporation, first aired November 17, 2002.
6. John Ydstie, "Complicated BMW," *All Things Considered*, August 8, 2002. An mp3 file is available here: www.cheesebikini.com/2002/08/09/all-things-considered-rips-bmw-idrive-interface/.

7. Dennis Crowley, "BMW iDrive = one of the worst designs in the history of products," *Flickr*, photograph taken November 21, 2007, www.flickr.com/photos/dpstyles/2052119037/.

8. Eric Seiden, "Suckitude: The Legacy of BMW's iDrive," *The Quagmire*, August 16, 2008, http://quagmire.darsys.net/2008/08/suckitude-legacy-of-bmws-idrive/.

9. Jakob Nielsen, "Why Consumer Products Have Inferior User Experience," Nielsen Norman Group, March 15, 2004, www.useit.com/alertbox/20040315.html.

10. Don Norman, "Interaction Design for Automobile Interiors," jnd.org, www.jnd.org/dn.mss/interaction_design_for_automobile_interiors.html.

11. Edward Loh, "Then and Now—BMW iDrive No Longer Sucks," *Truck Trend*, February 5, 2009, http://blogs.trucktrend.com/6441529/vehicle-accessories/then-and-now-bmw-idrive-no-longer-sucks/index.html#ixzz1UAS9B69k.

12. Karl Brauer, "Why iDrive Won't Fly," Edmunds.com, July 1, 2004, www.edmunds.com/car-news/why-idrive-wont-fly.html.

13. Aaron Robinson, "BMW 745i The Ultimate Interfacing Machine," *Car and Driver*, June 2002, www.caranddriver.com/reviews/bmw-745i-road-test.

14. James G. Cobb, "Menus Behaving Badly," *New York Times*, May 12, 2002, www.nytimes.com/2002/05/12/automobiles/menus-behaving-badly.html.

15. "Road Test 750Li V8," *Consumer Reports*, www.consumerreports.org/cro/bmw/7-series/road-test.htm.

16. Robert Farago, "BMW I Drive," *The Truth About Cars*, February 25, 2002, www.thetruthaboutcars.com/2002/02/bmw-i-drive/.

17. For an eloquent explanation, I recommend Jef Raskin, "Intuitive Equals Familiar," September 1994, www.asktog.com/papers/raskinintuit.html.

18. Norman, "Interaction Design for Automobile Interiors."

19. BMW 2002 745i/745Li Owner's Manual.

20. Nielsen, "Why Consumer Products Have Inferior User Experience."

21. R. B. Miller, "Response Time in Man-Computer Conversational Transactions," *Proceedings of the AFIPS Fall Joint Computer Conference* 33 (1968): 267–77.

22. David Yochum, "2008 BMW 760Li," *Automobile*, February 2009, www.automobilemag.com/reviews/editors_notebook/0806_2008_bmw_760li_luxury_sedan_review/idrive.html.

23. For example, see the credibility research at Stanford Persuasive Tech Lab, http://captology.stanford.edu.

24. Annie Rydström et al., "Multifunctional Systems in Vehicles: A Usability Evaluation," Proceedings of CybErg 2005: The Fourth International Cyberspace Conference on Ergonomics, p. 7, http://pure.ltu.se/portal/files/714949/Article.

25. Rydström et al., "Multifunctional Systems," 7.

26. David Zenlea, "2009 BMW 335d," *Automobile*, March 2009, www.automobilemag.com/green/reviews/0901_2009_bmw_335d_review/.

27. Winding Road Staff, "Buyer's Guide: Mid-Size Luxury Sedans," *Winding Road*, May 19, 2011, www.windingroad.com/articles/reviews/buyers-guide-mid-size-luxury-sedans/.

28. "Road Test 750Li V8," *Consumer Reports*.

29. Joe DeMatio, "2009 Hyundai Genesis V8," *Automobile*, February 2009, www.automobilemag.com/reviews/editors_notebook/0808_2008_hyundai_genesis_v8/.

30. Edward Loh, "Comparison: 2011 Ford Mustang GT vs. 2011 BMW M3 Coupe," *Motor Trend*, October 2010, www.motortrend.com/roadtests/coupes/1010_2011_2011_ford_mustang_gt_vs_2011_bmw_m3_comparison/viewall.html.

31. Loh, "Then and Now."

32. "Raining Luxury," *Automobile*.

33. Kevin Massy, "Tech Design Flaws Hit Mercedes, BMW, and Audi in J. D. Power's 2006 Study," *CNET*, June 19, 2006, http://reviews.cnet.com/8301-10921_7-6543837-4.html.

34. "BMW 7 Series," *Wikipedia*, last modified February 7, 2013, http://en.wikipedia.org/wiki/BMW_7_Series#Production_and_sales.

35. Ben Parr, "Google Wave: A Complete Guide," *Mashable*, May 28, 2009, http://mashable.com/2009/05/28/google-wave-guide/.

36. Oliver Wrede, "Thoughts on Google Wave," *details of a global brain*, August 2, 2009, http://wrede.interfacedesign.org/archives/1701.html.

37. Lars Rasmussen, "Went Walkabout. Brought Back Google Wave," *Google Official Blog*, May 28, 2009, http://googleblog.blogspot.com/2009/05/went-walkabout-brought-back-google-wave.html.

38. Ben Parr, "Could Google Wave Redefine Email and Web Communication?" *Mashable*, May 28, 2009, http://mashable.com/2009/05/28/google-wave/.

39. Robert Scoble, "Google Wave Crashes on Beach of Overhype," *Scobleizer*, October 1, 2009, http://scobleizer.com/2009/10/01/google-wave-crashes-on-beach-of-overhype/.

40. Louis Gray, "Google Wave Hits Shore. Flash Flood Warning in Effect," *louisgray.com*, October 1, 2009, http://blog.louisgray.com/2009/10/google-wave-hits-shore-flash-flood.html.

41. Morgan Missen, "Does Google Use Google Wave In-House?" *Quora*, August 1, 2010, www.quora.com/Does-Google-use-Google-Wave-in-house.

42. Urs Hölzle, "Update on Google Wave," *Google Official Blog*, August 4, 2010, http://googleblog.blogspot.com/2010/08/update-on-google-wave.html.

43. BMW 2002 745i/745Li Owner's Manual.

44. Rasmussen, "Went Walkabout."

45. "List of Countries by Traffic-Related Death Rate," *Wikipedia*, last modified February 4, 2013, http://en.wikipedia.org/wiki/List_of_countries_by_traffic-related_death_rate. Looking at road fatalities per 100,000 motor vehicles, the rate in Germany was 7.2 and the rate in the United States was 15.

46. For example, "Im eigentlichen Mittelpunkt steht aber der metallisch glänzende, zentral angeordnete Dreh-Drück-Steller des menügestützten Bediensystems iDrive. Das iDrive-System selbst ist - bis auf einige Ausnahmen - durchdacht und nach längerer Eingewöhnungszeit durchaus intuitiv zu handhaben," www.auto-motor-und-sport.de/einzeltests/bmw-bayerische-mutations-werke-767411.html.

47. Richard Read, "How Many Shoppers Skip the Test Drive? More Than You Think," *The Car Connection*, August 13, 2012, www.thecarconnection.com/news/1078435_how-many-shoppers-skip-the-test-drive-more-than-you-think?fbfanpage.

48. Frank Markus, "Technologue: iDrive Redux," *Motor Trend*, June 2005, www.motortrend.com/features/editorial/112_0506_technologue/viewall.html.

49. Loh, "Then and Now."

50. For example, see "BMW—Ideas Are Everything," July 16, 2008, www.youtube.com/watch?v=EOKKx-dbayo.

51. Rasmussen, "Went Walkabout."

52. Aaron Cheang, "Your Thoughts on Waving So Far," *Google Wave Blog*, November 27, 2009, http://googlewave.blogspot.com/2009/11/your-thoughts-on-waving-so-far.html.

53. MG Siegler, "Eric Schmidt on Google Wave's Death," August 4, 2010, www.youtube.com/watch?v=FJ-jNaAxISk. Incidentally, Google Wave technology did make its way into other products. The playback feature from Wave, for example, became the ripples feature in Google Plus.

54. Ezra Dyer, "A Full-Size Upgrade from Dodge at No Additional Charge," *New York Times*, February 10, 2012, www.nytimes.com/2012/02/12/automobiles/charger-a-full-size-upgrade-from-dodge.html.

55. NHTSA, "Visual-Manual NIITSA Driver Distraction Guidelines for In-Vehicle Electronic Devices," February 24, 2012, www.federalregister.gov/articles/2012/02/24/2012-4017/visual-manual-nhtsa-driver-distraction-guidelines-for-in-vehicle-electronic-devices#p-537.

56. NHTSA, "Visual-Manual." Although the report's authors conceded that "no general consensus exists as to the threshold at which an absolute level of distraction due to a driver performing a task becomes unacceptably high," they nevertheless chose a reference task that all drivers should be capable of performing without causing driving distraction: manual radio tuning.

Chapter 3

1. Steve Krug, *Don't Make Me Think* (Berkeley, CA: New Riders, 2005). This classic of the field is an excellent introductory book about Web usability.

2. Beverly Freeman, "Yahoo! OpenID: One Key, Many Doors. OpenID User Experience Research," *Yahoo!*, July 2008, http://developer.yahoo.com/openid/openid-research-jul08.pdf. The Yahoo! test report refers to OpenID's original user interface.

3. Tom Hughes-Croucher, "Yahoo! Releases OpenID Research," *Yahoo! Developer Network Blog*, October 14, 2008, http://developer.yahoo.com/blogs/ydn/posts/2008/10/open_id_research/.

4. Example URIs courtesy of Jeff Atwood, "Does the World Really Need Yet Another Username and Password?" *Coding Horror*, May 28, 2008, www.codinghorror.com/blog/2008/05/openid-does-the-world-really-need-yet-another-username-and-password.html.

5. For an explanation of this use of memory and a suggestion to rephrase this as "Cued recall rather than free recall," see Dr. Dinesh Katre, "Paraphrasing the Heuristic 'Recognition Than Recall'," *Journal of HC*, May 2006, www.hceye.org/UsabilityInsights/?p=37.

6. Eric Sachs, "Google Federated Login Research," https://docs.google.com/present/view?skipauth=true&pli=1&id=ajkhp5hpp3tt_43hssxgp6g.

7. Max Engel, "MySpaceID Usability Testing," *MySpace*, February 9, 2009, www.slideshare.net/maxengel/myspaceid-usability-testing.

8. "What's Wrong with OpenID?" *Quora*, www.quora.com/OpenID/What-s-wrong-with-OpenID.

9. "We'll Be Retiring Our Support of OpenID on May 1 [2011]," *37Signals Product Blog*, January 25, 2011, http://productblogarchive.37signals.com/products/2011/01/well-be-retiring-our-support-of-openid-on-may-1.html.

10. Rob Conery, "Open ID Is a Nightmare," *WekeRoad*, November 17, 2010, http://blog.wekeroad.com/thoughts/open-id-is-a-party-that-happened.

11. "What's Wrong with OpenID?"

12. Charlie Cheever, "How, If at All, Is Facebook Connect Better Than OpenID?" *Quora*, July 18, 2010, www.quora.com/How-if-at-all-is-Facebook-Connect-better-than-OpenID.

13. Jennifer Van Grove, "Each Month 250 Million People Use Facebook Connect on the Web," *Mashable*, December 8, 2010, http://mashable.com/2010/12/08/facebook-connect-stats/.

14. "Adoption Committee," *OpenID Wiki*, last edited by Daniel Jacobson on February 16, 2010, http://wiki.openid.net/w/page/12995183/Adoption%20Committee.

15. Max Engel, "MySpaceID Usability Testing."

16. OpenID Foundation board member Chris Messina outlines the problems in "OpenID Usability Is Not an Oxymoron," *FactoryCity*, October 28, 2008, http://factoryjoe.com/blog/2008/10/28/openid-usability-is-not-an-oxymoron/.

17. Here's the math if you're curious: 1 billion divided by 5 equals 200,000,000 individuals, times 2 minutes is 400,000,000 minutes, divided by the 60 minutes in an hour is 6,666,666.66666667 hours, divided by the 24 hours in a day is 277,777.777777778 days, and divided by the 365 days in a year is 761.035007610351 years.

18. Chris Messina, "Perception and Reality in the Land of OpenID," *FactoryCity*, January 4, 2009, http://factoryjoe.com/blog/2009/01/04/perception-and-reality-in-the-land-of-openid/.

19. Chris Messina, "Interview with Don Thibeau, OIDF's Executive Director," *OpenID*, August 10, 2009, http://openid.net/2009/08/10/interview-with-don-thibeau-oidfs-executive-director/.

20. Chris Messina, "Where Should the OpenID Foundation Go in 2011?" *Chris Messina Blog*, November 29, 2010, http://chrismessina.me/b?page=2&group=text.

21. "We'll Be Retiring Our Support of OpenID," *37Signals Product Blog*.

22. OpenID Foundation, "What Is OpenID?" http://openid.net/get-an-openid/what-is-openid/.

Chapter 4

1. "Wesabe," *Crunchbase.com*, last edited February 17, 2012, www.crunchbase.com/company/wesabe.

2. Marc Hedlund, "Why Wesabe Lost to Mint," *Marc Hedlund's Blog*, http://blog.precipice.org/why-wesabe-lost-to-mint.

3. Jane J. Kim, "Managing Your Money in Public View," *Wall Street Journal*, June 14, 2007, http://online.wsj.com/article/SB118177906703834565.html.

4. Marc Hedlund, "Making the Web into a Banking Platform (Whether They Like It or Not)," *O'Reilly Radar*, July 25, 2007, http://radar.oreilly.com/2007/07/making-the-web-into-a-banking.html.

5. DeVer Warner, "Wesabe's Two Big Moves," comment posted on *AVC*, July 25, 2007, www.avc.com/a_vc/2007/07/wesabes-two-big.html?cid=77142036#comment-6a00d83451b2c969e200e55022899f8833.

6. Notebook Review Staff, "Wesabe Review," *Notebook Review*, July 14, 2009, www.notebookreview.com/default.asp?newsID=5134&review=Wesabe+Review.

7. Marc Hedlund, "Make Wesabe Better," a comment on *Wesabe Groups*, www.wesabe.com/groups/3-make-wesabe-better/discussions/410-are-you-worried-about-mint#comment_5897. This site was taken offline as of 2013.

8. Hedlund, "Why Wesabe Lost to Mint."

9. Jim Bruene, "Venture Funding Flows to Wesabe and Prosper; Wesabe Launches on Facebook," *NetBanker*, June 20, 2007, www.netbanker.com/2007/06/venture_funding_flows_to_wesab_prosper_wesabe_launches_facebook.html.

10. Amy Shuen, *Web 2.0: A Strategy Guide: Business Thinking and Strategies behind Successful Web 2.0 Implementations* (Sebastopol, CA: O'Reilly, 2008), 13–14.

11. Hedlund, "Making the Web into a Banking Platform."

12. Debbie Pfeifer, "Delta Community Credit Union Selects Wesabe Springboard(TM) for Money Management Tools and Community," *Bloomberg*, a Wesabe press release, April 28, 2009, www.bloomberg.com/apps/news?pid=newsarchive&sid=aT98_JZWOb9w; Colin Henderson, "Wesabe Today Announce That Palo Alto-Based Addison Avenue Federal Credit Union Is to Integrate Springboard Community App," *The Bankwatch*, July 13, 2009, http://thebankwatch.com/2009/07/13/wesabe-today-announce-that-palo-alto-based-addison-avenue-federal-credit-union-is-to-integrate-springboard-community-app/.

13. Michael Arrington, "More Money for Wesabe," *TechCrunch*, June 20, 2007, http://techcrunch.com/2007/06/20/more-money-for-wesabe/.

14. Tim O'Reilly, "What Is Web 2.0," *O'Reilly.com*, September 30, 2005, http://oreilly.com/web2/archive/what-is-web-20.html.

15. See Stanford Web Credibility Research, http://credibility.stanford.edu.
16. Eric Mattson, "Welcome to Wesabe, a New NetBanker.com Sponsor," *NetBanker*, December 11, 2009, www.netbanker.com/2009/12/welcome_to_wesabe_a_new_netbankercom_sponsor.html.
17. Poornima Vijayashanker, "Timeline: Mint.com—2009," *Femgineer*, January 4, 2010, http://femgineer.com/2010/01/timeline-mint-com-2009/.
18. Marc Hedlund, "Wesabe Is Discontinuing Its Accounts Tab as of July 31st," *The Wesabe Blog*, June 30, 2010, http://wesabe.wordpress.com/2010/06/30/wesabe-is-discontinuing-its-accounts-tab-as-of-july-31st/.
19. Hedlund, "Why Wesabe Lost to Mint."
20. Ibid.
21. Ibid.

Chapter 5

1. "The Walkman Effect," *Wikipedia*, last modified December 21, 2012, http://en.wikipedia.org/wiki/Walkman_effect.
2. "Microsoft Zune Love," *Amplicate*, http://amplicate.com/love/zune.
3. Walter S. Mossberg, "Microsoft's Zune Challenges iPod," *Wall Street Journal*, November 9, 2006, http://online.wsj.com/public/article/SB116302848393917854-wNNFl42I1SSNBP6dH5xF08kTRlQ_20071108.html?mod=blogs.
4. David Pogue, "Trying Out the Zune: iPod It's Not," *New York Times*, November 9, 2006, www.nytimes.com/2006/11/09/technology/09pogue.html.
5. Nate Anderson, "Microsoft Zune," *Ars Technica*, November 15, 2006, http://arstechnica.com/gadgets/2006/11/zune/.
6. David Pogue, "A New Zune for Serious Music Fans," *New York Times*, September 17, 2008, www.nytimes.com/2008/09/18/technology/personaltech/18pogue.html.
7. David Pogue, "Tuning In a Zippier Zune," *New York Times*, September 16, 2009, www.nytimes.com/2009/09/17/technology/personaltech/17pogue.html.
8. Katherine Boehret, "Microsoft Packs the New Zune HD with Bells, Whistles and Plenty of Style," *All Things D*, September 22, 2009, http://allthingsd.com/20090922/microsoft-packsthe-new-zune-hdwith-bells-whistlesand-plenty-of-style/.
9. Donald Bell, "Zune HD Review," *CNET*, September 17, 2009, http://reviews.cnet.com/mp3-players/zune-hd-32gb-platinum/4505-6490_7-33665869.html.
10. Microsoft Corporation, Form 10-K for the Fiscal Year Ended June 30, 2007 (filed August 3, 2007), p. 26, www.sec.gov/Archives/edgar/data/789019/000119312507170817/d10k.htm.
11 Microsoft Corporation, Form 10-K for the Fiscal Year Ended June 30, 2008 (filed July 31, 2008), www.sec.gov/Archives/edgar/data/789019/000119312508162768/d10k.htm.
12. Microsoft Corporation, Form 10-K for the Fiscal Year Ended June 30, 2009 (filed July 29, 2009), p. 28, www.sec.gov/Archives/edgar/data/789019/000119312509158735/d10k.htm; Microsoft Corporation, Form 10-K for the Fiscal Year Ended June 30, 2010 (filed July 30, 2010), p. 29, www.sec.gov/Archives/edgar/data/789019/000119312510171791/d10k.htm; Microsoft Corporation, Form 10-K for the Fiscal Year Ended June 30, 2011 (filed July 28, 2011), p. 30, www.sec.gov/Archives/edgar/data/789019/000119312511200680/d10k.htm.
13. "Zune: Top Issues," *Xbox*, www.zune.net/en-US/support/zuneplayers/supportzuneplayers.htm.
14. "Apple Reports First Quarter Results," Apple, January 24, 2012, www.apple.com/pr/library/2012/01/24Apple-Reports-First-Quarter-Results.html.
15. Don Norman, *Emotional Design: Why We Love (or Hate) Everyday Things* (New York: Basic Books, 2004), 83–84.

16. Robert Scoble, "My Thoughts about Zune vs. iPod," *Scobleizer*, October 26, 2006, http://scobleizer.com/2006/10/26/my-thoughts-about-zune-vs-ipod/.
17. Anil Dash, "The Problem Is, the Zune Is Brown," *A Blog About Making Culture*, November 14, 2006, http://dashes.com/anil/2006/11/brown-zune.html.
18. Pogue, "Tuning In a Zippier Zune."
19. Dean Takahashi, "The Making of the Xbox: Microsoft's Journey to the Next Generation (Part 2)," *VentureBeat*, November 15, 2011, http://venturebeat.com/2011/11/15/the-making-of-the-xbox-part-2/.
20. "Console Wars," *Wikipedia*, last modified February 22, 2013, http://en.wikipedia.org/wiki/Console_wars.
21. "Every Gaming System Has Its Fans, but Women Like Wii," *nielsenwire*, February 17, 2009, http://blog.nielsen.com/nielsenwire/consumer/every-gaming-system-has-its-fans-but-women-like-wii/.
22. Microsoft Corporation, Form 10-K for the Fiscal Year Ended June 30, 2009. There is no publicly available development cost, but we can infer rough estimates from securities documents. For example, Microsoft's earning release for the quarter ending June 2009 alone showed a loss of $130 million, "primarily reflecting decreased Zune and PC hardware product revenue."

Chapter 6

1. Jon Udell, "Critical Mass and Social Network Fatigue," *Jon Udell* (blog), February 6, 2007, http://blog.jonudell.net/2007/02/06/critical-mass-and-social-network-fatigue/.
2. David Card, "The Next Wave of Social Media Nears Critical Mass," *GigaOM*, November 8, 2010, http://gigaom.com/2010/11/08/the-next-wave-of-social-media-nears-critical-mass/; "Critical Mass (Sociodynamics)," *Wikipedia*, last modified February 9, 2013, http://en.wikipedia.org/wiki/Critical_mass_(sociodynamics).
3. Megan McCarthy, "Pownce Raises Angel Funding," *Wired*, February 1, 2008, www.wired.com/business/2008/02/pownce-raises-a/.
4. Jeremiah Owyang, "Keeping Track of the Pownce Reviews," *Web Strategy*, June 30, 2007, www.web-strategist.com/blog/2007/06/30/keeping-track-of-the-pownce-reviews/.
5. Michael Muchmore, "Site of the Week: Pownce," *PC Magazine*, September 11, 2007, www.pcmag.com/article2/0,2817,2181971,00.asp.
6. Rafe Needleman, "First Look at Pownce," *CNET*, June 27, 2007, http://news.cnet.com/8301-17939_109-9736178-2.html.
7. Michael Arrington, "Kevin v. Evan," *TechCrunch*, July 1 2007, http://techcrunch.com/2007/07/01/kevin-v-evan/.
8. Twitter, Crunchbase Profile, www.crunchbase.com/company/twitter.
9. Daniel Burka (Pownce co-founder), personal correspondence with the author, April 30, 2012.
10. Michael Arrington, "Is Pownce Going to the DeadPool?" *TechCrunch*, December 20, 2007, http://techcrunch.com/2007/12/20/is-pownce-going-to-the-deadpool/.
11. Paul Stamatiou, "Review: The Pownce.FM You'll Never See," *Hi, I'm Paul Stamatiou* (blog), n.d., http://paulstamatiou.com/review-the-powncefm-youll-never-see.
12. Taylor Dewey et al., "The Impact of Social Media on Social Unrest in the Arab Spring," (report prepared for the Defense Intelligence Agency), Stanford University, March 20, 2012, http://publicpolicy.stanford.edu/system/files/SocialMedia_FINAL%2020%20Mar.pdf.

Chapter 7

1. "Don't be evil" is an unofficial motto of Google. See "Don't Be Evil," *Wikipedia*, last modified February 6, 2013, http://en.wikipedia.org/wiki/Don't_be_evil.
2. "AIGA Standards of Professional Practice," AIGA, 1994, www.aiga.org/standards-professional-practice/.
3. David Evans, "Graduating from Classmates.com," *Flip the Media* (blog), March 4, 2011, http://flipthemedia.com/index.php/2011/03/graduating-from-classmates-com/.
4. Tom Spring, "Just Cancel the @#%$* Account!" *PCWorld*, December 22, 2006, www.pcworld.com/article/128206/article.html.
5. Betsy Schiffman, "Classmates.com IPO: What Are These People Thinking?" *Wired*, November 30, 2007, www.wired.com/epicenter/2007/11/is-classmatesco/.
6. Customer service phone call script, Webloyalty, October 21, 2008, www.benedelman.org/posttransaction/d4.pdf.
7. Jeff Nolan, "The 'Piss Off Your Prospects Enough That They Sign Up' Sales Model," *Venture Chronicles* (blog), March 22, 2006, http://jeffnolan.com/wp/2006/03/22/the-piss-off-your-prospects-enough-that-they-sign-up-sales-model/.
8. "Plaxo Hate," *Amplicate*, http://amplicate.com/hate/plaxo.
9. Russell Glitman, "Plaxo Contacts," *PC Magazine*, March 19, 2003, www.pcmag.com/article2/0,2817,940255,00.asp.
10. David Coursey, "Why My Address Book Is Spamming You," *ZDNet*, December 8, 2003, http://web.archive.org/web/20070105030148/http://review.zdnet.com/AnchorDesk/4520-7297_16-5111563.html.
11. Michael Arrington, "Plaxo: Now With Less Evil," *TechCrunch*, March 22, 2006, http://techcrunch.com/2006/03/22/plaxo-now-with-less-evil/.
12. Michael Arrington, "The Plaxo Virus," *Crunch Notes* (blog), January 3, 2006, www.crunchnotes.com/2006/01/03/the-plaxo-virus/.
13. Preston Smalley, personal communication with the author, December 8, 2011.
14. Ibid.
15. Redgee Capili, "A Little Less in Your Inbox," *Plaxo Blog*, March 20, 2006, http://blog.plaxo.com/2006/03/a_little_less_i/.
16. Arrington, "Plaxo: Now With Less Evil."
17. Ben Golub, "An Apology," *Plaxo Blog*, March 24, 2006, http://blog.plaxo.com/2006/03/an_apology/.
18. John McCrea, personal communication with the author, May 24, 2012.

Chapter 8

1. While this engineering feat results in a sleeker design that will more easily fit in your pocket, it may also be regarded as a customer experience setback because the signal quality is not as good as with a traditional antenna.
2. Chris Ziegler, "Nokia 5800 XpressMusic Review," *Engadget*, March 30, 2009, www.engadget.com/2009/03/30/nokia-5800-xpressmusic-review/.
3. Vincent Nguyen, "Nokia N97 Review," article retrieved from http://web.archive.org/web/20111016160734/http://www.phonemag.com/nokia-n97-review-069300.php.
4. John Blackburn, "A Closer Look at iPhone Transition Animations," *Watching Apple* (blog), November 19, 2009, http://watchingapple.com/2009/11/a-closer-look-at-iphone-transition-animations/.
5. Dave Stevenson, "Nokia X6 Review," *TechRadar*, December 7, 2009, www.techradar.com/us/reviews/phones/mobile-phones/nokia-x6-656297/review.
6. R. B. Miller, "Response Time in Man-Computer Conversational Transactions," *Proceedings of the AFIPS Fall Joint Computer Conference* 33 (1968): 267–77.

7. Paul Skidmore was one of the first to notice the "iOS-ification of OS X." See Paul Skidmore, "I've Seen the Future of iOS and OS X, and It Starts with iLife," *Macgasm*, February 8, 2012, www.macgasm.net/2012/02/08/future-ios-os-starts-ilife/.

8. Michael Friedman, "7 Professional Editors Share Their FCPX Experiences," *Philip Bloom* (blog), February 7, 2012, http://philipbloom.net/2012/02/07/fcpxeditors/.

9. Ibid.

10. Ibid.

11. David Pogue, "Professional Video Editors Weigh In on Final Cut Pro X," *New York Times*, June 23, 2011, http://pogue.blogs.nytimes.com/2011/06/23/professional-video-editors-weigh-in-on-final-cut-pro-x/.

12. Dan Radovsky, "Last Call for Final Cut? Part 2," *The Motley Fool*, January 28, 2012, www.fool.com/investing/general/2012/01/28/last-call-for-final-cut-part-2.aspx?source=isesitlnk0000001&mrr=0.50.

13. Richard Harrington, "My Response to David Pogue's 'Professional Video Editors Weigh In on Final Cut Pro X'," *Richard Harrington* (blog), June 24, 2011, www.richardharringtonblog.com/files/fcpx_response.php.

14. Paul Skidmore, "The Naked Truth about Final Cut Pro 10.0.3, and Where It Stands Today," *Macgasm*, February 6, 2012, www.macgasm.net/2012/02/06/thoughts-fcpx-thinking-warning-post-nudity-linkbait/.

15. Michael Muchmore, "Apple Final Cut Pro X 10.0.3," *PC Magazine*, February 7, 2012, www.pcmag.com/article2/0,2817,2388456,00.asp.

16. Matt Jones, "Lost Futures: Unconscious Gestures?" *Magic Nihilism* (blog), November 15, 2007, http://magicalnihilism.com/2007/11/15/lost-futures-unconscious-gestures/.

17. Victor Lombardi, "The Evolving Homepage: The Growth of Three Booksellers," *Boxes and Arrows*, March 11, 2002, http://boxesandarrows.com/view/the_evolving_homepage_the_growth_of_three_booksellers.

18. Gerald L. Lohse, Eric J. Johnson, and Steven Bellman, "Cognitive Lock-In and the Power Law of Practice," *Journal of Marketing* 67 (April 2003): 6275, http://papers.ssrn.com/sol3/papers.cfm?abstract_id=1324766.

19. An extreme example is the writer William F. Buckley Jr.'s affection for the WordStar word processing software. He continued to use the software long after development was discontinued. Of it he said, "I'm told there are better programs, but I'm also told there are better alphabets." See Jamie Murphy, "Computers: A Convert to the Write Stuff," *Time*, June 21, 2005, www.time.com/time/magazine/article/0,9171,1074867,00.html.

Chapter 9

1. Tim Ocock, "Guest Post: Symbian OS—One of the Most Successful Failures in Tech History," *TechCrunch*, November 8, 2010, http://techcrunch.com/2010/11/08/guest-post-symbian-os-one-of-the-most-successful-failures-in-tech-history-2/.

2. Bruce Sterling, "Dead Media Beat: Symbian OS, One of the Most Successful Failures in Tech History," *Wired*, November 11, 2010, www.wired.com/beyond_the_beyond/2010/11/dead-media-beat-symbian-os-one-of-the-most-successful-failures-in-tech-history/#comments.

3. "General Aviation Safety Record—Current and Historic," Aircraft Owners and Pilots Association, March 2011, www.aopa.org/whatsnew/stats/safety.html.

4. Kathryn Schulz, *Being Wrong: Adventures in the Margin of Error* (New York: Ecco, 2011), 304–5.

5. For more discussion of these phenomena in business, see Max H. Bazerman and Ann E. Tenbrunsel, *Blind Spots: Why We Fail to Do What's Right and What to Do about It* (Princeton, NJ: Princeton University Press, 2011). As applied to experience design, see Joe Lamantia, "Designing Ethical Experiences: Understanding Juicy Rationalizations," *UXmatters*, June 23, 2008, www.uxmatters.com/ mt/archives/2008/06/designing-ethical-experiences-understanding-juicy-rationalizations.php.

6. Chana Joffe-Walt, "Can Eurozone Countries Actually Follow Their Own Rules This Time?" *NPR*, December 7, 2011, www.npr.org/blogs/money/2011/12/07/143274540/ can-eurozone-countries-actually-follow-their-own-rules-this-time.

7. John Branch, "Snow Fall: The Avalanche at Tunnel Creek," *New York Times*, December 2012, www.nytimes.com/projects/2012/ snow-fall/#/?part=tunnel-creek.

8. Scott Berkun, "Microsoft and Creative Destruction," *Scott Berkun* (blog), February 11, 2010, http://scottberkun.com/2010/microsoft-and-creative-destruction/.

9. NPR Staff, "Failure: The F-Word Silicon Valley Loves and Hates," *NPR*, June 19, 2012, www.npr.org/2012/06/19/155005546/ failure-the-f-word-silicon-valley-loves-and-hates.

10. Bruce Springsteen, "Exclusive: The Complete Text of Bruce Springsteen's SXSW Keynote Address," *Rolling Stone*, March 28, 2012, www.rollingstone.com/ music/news/exclusive-the-complete-text-of-bruce-springsteens-sxsw-keynote-address-20120328.

Chapter 10

1. Evidence to substantiate this timing is difficult to find and debatable, but I think the 1980s, with the emergence of mice and windows and the efforts of designers at companies such as Xerox and Apple, mark the "widespread" use of user-centered design.

2. "Agile Software Development," *Wikipedia*, last modified March 20, 2013, http://en.wikipedia.org/wiki/Agile_software_development.

3. Kent Beck et al., "Manifesto for Agile Software Development," http://agilemanifesto.org.

4. Zenas Block and Ian C. MacMillan, "Milestones for Successful Venture Planning," *Harvard Business Review* (September 1985), http://hbr.org/1985/09/ milestones-for-successful-venture-planning/ar/1.

5. Clayton M. Christensen, *The Innovator's Dilemma* (New York: HarperCollins, 2000), 180–81. Interestingly, Christensen points out in the Introduction that this classic book is essentially about failure.

6. Rita McGrath and Ian MacMillan, "Discovery-Driven Planning," *Harvard Business Review* 73, no. 4 (July 1995): 44–54.

7. Steven Gary Blank, *The Four Steps to the Epiphany: Successful Strategies for Products that Win* (Louisville, KY: CafePress, 2005).

8. Steve Blank, "The Customer Development Manifesto: Reasons for the Revolution," *Steve Blank* (blog), September 3, 2009, http://steveblank.com/2009/09/03/ the-customer-development-manifesto-reasons-for-the-revolution-part-2/.

9. Eric Ries, "What Is Customer Development?" *Startup Lessons Learned* (blog), November 8, 2008, www.startuplessonslearned.com/2008/11/what-is-customer-development.html.

10. Eric Ries, *The Lean Startup: How Today's Entrepreneurs Use Continuous Innovation to Create Radically Successful Businesses* (New York: Crown Business, 2011).

11. Ben R. Rich and Leo Janos, *Skunk Works: A Personal Memoir of My Years at Lockheed* (New York: Back Bay Books, 1996).

12. Vijay Pattni, "Meet the Brains behind the Toyota GT 86," *TopGear*, January 3, 2013, www.topgear.com/uk/photos/toyota-gt-86-tetsuya-tada-yoshinori-sasaki-2012-08-24.
13. Fred Wilson, "MBA Tuesday," *AVC* (blog), February 16, 2011, www.avc.com/a_vc/2011/02/mba-tuesday.html.
14. Scott Anthony, "The Masters of Innovation," *HBR Blog Network*, March 23, 2012, http://hbr.org/web/slideshows/the-masters-of-innovation/1-blank.
15. Wilson, "MBA Tuesday."

Credits

1.1: Analise, "bloomberg terminal.jpg," Flickr, photograph taken July 17, 2008, www.flickr.com/photos/lisey/2680032851/. Used with permission. **1.2:** www.zocdoc.com. **1.3:** From Howard Wainer, *Graphic Discovery: A Trout in the Milk and Other Visual Adventures* (Princeton, NJ: Princeton University Press, 2005), 148. **1.4:** "Coalition: Vast Majority of Iraqis Still Alive," *The Onion*, June 23, 2004, www.theonion.com/articles/coalition-vast-majority-of-iraqis-still-alive,1185/. **1.5:** Minnesota Department of Transportation, Interstate 35W Bridge in Minneapolis, August 2, 2007, www.dot.state.mn.us/i35wbridge/photos/aerial/aug-2/images/35W%20bridge%201%20212_jpg.jpg. **1.6:** Thomaswm, "Metz_VH48.jpg," Wikipedia, photograph taken January 21, 2006, http://en.wikipedia.org/wiki/File:Metz_VH48_v2.jpg. **1.7:** Mike Gikas, "Lab Tests: Why Consumer Reports Can't Recommend the iPhone 4," *Consumer Reports*, July 12, 2010, http://news.consumerreports.org/electronics/2010/07/apple-iphone-4-antenna-issue-iphone4-problems-dropped-calls-lab-test-confirmed-problem-issues-signal-strength-att-network-gsm.html. **1.9:** "Lamborghini Urus Concept—Lambo SUV Revealed," *Road & Track*, April 22, 2012, www.youtube.com/watch?v=iUjRq6YfqCQ. **1.10:** Phil Price Rally School, "Phil Price Rally School In-Car," May 26, 2010, www.youtube.com/watch?v=NCL6xXzyiTA. **1.11:** Victor Lombardi, "The Ribbon from Microsoft Office 2007," July 31, 2012, www.youtube.com/watch?v=LAVZUaMdwp0. **1.12:** "Drupal Accessibility User Testing Compilation," April 19, 2010, www.youtube.com/watch?v=cMlzQRdA9tE. **1.13:** Evan-Amos, "File:Sony-wm-fx421-walkman.jpg," Wikimedia Commons, September 5, 2010, http://commons.wikimedia.org/wiki/File:Sony-wm-fx421-walkman.jpg. **1.14:** Apple, "Apple iPod Touch," 2012, http://store.apple.com/us/browse/home/shop_ipod/family/ipod_touch.

2.1: Liftarn, "1902OldsmobileCurvedDash.jpg," Wikimedia Commons, August 30, 2009, http://commons.wikimedia.org/wiki/File:1902OldsmobileCurvedDash.jpg. **2.2:** decampos, "Aston Martin Lagonda cluster," Flickr, photograph taken November 20, 2006, www.flickr.com/photos/7977458@N08/5858192558/. Used by permission. **2.3:** "125749_Interior_T.jpg", Barrett-Jackson Auction Company, www.barrett-jackson.com/application/onlinesubmission/lotdetails.aspx?ln=21&aid=463. **2.4:** EricS, "Idrive-Controller.jpg," Wikimedia Commons, January 30, 2005, http://commons.wikimedia.org/wiki/File:Idrive-Controller.jpg. **2.5:** BMW, http://bmw.com. **2.6:** From Annie Rydström, Peter Bengtsson, Camilla Grane, Robert Broström, Johannes Agardh, and Jennie Nilsson, "Multifunctional Systems in Vehicles: A Usability Evaluation," p. 5. In A. Thatcher, J. James, and A. Todd, *Proceedings of CybErg 2005, The Fourth International Cyberspace Conference on Ergonomics* (Johannesburg: International Ergonomics Association Press, 2005), http://pure.ltu.se/portal/files/714949/Article. **2.7:** Ibid., 6. **2.8:** BMW, http://bmw.com. **2.10:** plien, "IDrive BMW Z4 E89.jpg," Wikimedia Commons, 2009, http://commons.wikimedia.org/wiki/File:IDrive_BMW_Z4_E89.jpg. **2.11:** Data from "BMW 7 Series: Production and Sales," Wikipedia, February 7, 2013, http://en.wikipedia.org/wiki/BMW_7_Series#Production_and_sales. **2.12:** "Google Wave.png," Wikipedia, screenshot taken by "User:Zayani," June 28, 2010, http://en.wikipedia.org/wiki/File:Google_Wave.png. **2.13:** Google Wave, "Getting Started with Google Wave," May 18, 2010, www.youtube.com/watch?v=eKUAqNGVwX0. **2.14:** "Google Wave.png," Wikipedia, screenshot taken by "User:Zayani," June 28, 2010, http://en.wikipedia.org/wiki/File:Google_Wave.png. **2.15:** Colin Zhu, "Google Wave Invitations," Flickr, screenshot taken October 14, 2009, www.flickr.com/photos/colinzhu/4010539433/. **2.16:** MG Siegler, "Google Wave: There Will Be Backlash," *Techcrunch*, September 30, 2009, http://techcrunch.com/2009/09/30/google-wave-there-will-be-backlash/. **2.17:** EasierToUnderstandThanWave.com, image retrieved from www.flickr.com/photos/43219336@N03/4003600473/. **2.18:** Ryan Tate, "Google Wave Dead after Two Months," *Gawker*, August 4, 2010, http://gawker.com/5604846/

google-wave-dead-after-two-months. **2.19:** MG Siegler, "Eric Schmidt on Google Wave's Death," August 4, 2010, www.youtube.com/watch?v=FJ-jNaAxISk.

3.1: Chris Messina, "Yahoo! OpenID Summary," Flickr, January 18, 2008, www.flckr.com/photos/factoryjoe/2202173237/. **3.2:** "Start Using Your OpenID," OpenID Foundation, http://openid.net/get-an-openid/start-using-your-openid/. **3.3:** Symantec, https://pip.verisignlabs.com/register.do;jsessionid=4EDD48942F42A 2213FD5B4A889CB14C8.pip3. **3.4:** Symantec, https://pip.verisignlabs.com/login.do. **3.5:** StackExchange, http://stackexchange.com/users/login?returnurl=%2f. **3.6:** Twitterfeed, http://twitterfeed.com/session/new. **3.7:** Alex Sharp, "Useful Login Form UI PSD", http://ui-cloud.com/useful-login-form-ui-psd/. **3.8, 3.9:** Vimeo, https://vimeo.com/log_in. **3.10a,b:** Winding Road, www.windingroad.com/articles/news/zero-unveils-2012-electric-motorcycle-lineup/. **3.12a,b:** Plaxo, www.plaxo.com.

4.1: Colin Henderson, "screenshot-7.png," The Bankwatch, April 24, 2008, http://bankwatch.files.wordpress.com/2008/04/screenshot-7.png. **4.2:** Wesabe, Wesabe Uploader, https://wesabe.com. **4.3:** Wesabe, Wesabe Firefox Browser Extension. **4.4:** Alexa, www.alexa.com/siteinfo/wesabe.com. **4.5a:** Mint.com, wwws.mint.com/overview.event. **4.5b:** Mint.com, wwws.mint.com/trend.event. **4.6:** Wesabe, www.wesabe.com/groups/. **4.7:** IntoMobile, www.intomobile.com/2009/05/12/wesabes-free-iphone-app-lets-users-manager-their-money-on-the-go/. **4.8:** Mint.com, www.mint.com/blog/updates/mint-iphone-app/.

5.1: Toshiba, http://gigabeat.com. **5.2:** Microsoft, http://microsoft.com/zune. **5.3:** Apple, www.apple.com/ipod/. **5.4:** Microsoft, http://microsoft.com/zune. **5.5:** Based on data from Daniel Eran Dilger, "Zune Sales Still in the Toilet," *RoughlyDrafted Magazine*, May 9, 2008, www.roughlydrafted.com/2008/05/09/zune-sales-still-in-the-toilet/. **5.6:** Apple, www.apple.com/pr/. **5.7:** Toy by Publications International, Ltd. From the collection of Anna Lombardi. Photograph by the author. **5.8:** Courtesy of Marlena, www.etsy.com/listing/88000467/ipod-earphones-headphones-earrings-apple. **5.9:** Microsoft, http://press.xbox360.com.

6.1: Mick Liubinskas, "Pownce: mick l," Flickr, photograph taken July 11, 2007, www.flickr.com/photos/adventures/783757076/. Used with a Creative Commons license. **6.2:** Bull3t Hughes, "Pownce Desktop Application," Flickr, photograph taken July 7, 2007, www.flickr.com/photos/bull3t/745745011/. Used with a Creative Commons license. **6.3:** Pownce, http://pownce.com. **6.4:** Joakim Jardenberg, "twitter," Flickr, photograph taken April 12, 2007, www.flickr.com/photos/jocke66/456537540/. Used with a Creative Commons license. **6.5:** Twitter, http://twitter.com. **6.6:** Michael Arrington, "Is Pownce Going to the DeadPool?" *TechCrunch*, December 20, 2007, http://techcrunch.com/2007/12/20/is-pownce-going-to-the-deadpool/. **6.7:** Paul Stamatiou, "pownce_fm_public_songs_1100.jpg," http://turbo.paulstamatiou.com/uploads/2008/05/pownce_fm_public_songs_1100.jpg. **6.8, 6.9:** Compete.com, www.compete.com/us/.

7.1: Classmates, http://classmates.com. **7.2:** Sandi Hardmeier, "image_c884427b-da16-4049-a5fa-c50a2a875c44.png," Spyware Sucks, March 23, 2008, www.msmvps.com/blogs/spywaresucks/archive/2008/03/23/1550824.aspx. **7.3:** Classmates, http://classmates.com. **7.4:** Technorati, http://technorati.com. **7.5:** Classmates, http://classmates.com. **7.6:** JR Raphael, "5 Reasons I Hope Classmates.com Gets Sued into Oblivion," *PCWorld*, November 12, 2008, www.pcworld.com/article/153769/classmates_suit.html. **7.7:** Classmates, http://classmates.com. **7.8, 7.9:** Plaxo, www.plaxo.com. **7.10:** Dave Taylor, "Can I Get Plaxo Spam?" *Ask Dave Taylor!*, December 14, 2005, www.askdavetaylor.com/can_i_get_plaxo_spam.html. **7.11:** GoodContacts,

GoodContacts for Outlook. **7.12:** Plaxo, Plaxo toolbar for Microsoft Outlook. **7.13:** Ben Golub, "An Apology," Plaxo Blog, March 24, 2006, http://blog.plaxo.com/2006/03/an_apology/.

8.1: Nokia, www.nokia.com. **8.2:** "Nokia-8810.jpg," Wikipedia, November 9, 2011, http://en.wikipedia.org/wiki/File:Nokia-8810.jpg. **8.3:** JosefKolar, "Symbian-s60-hotmail.jpg," Wikipedia, 2011, http://en.wikipedia.org/wiki/File:Symbian-s60-hotmail.jpg. Used with a Creative Commons license. **8.4a:** Shritwod, "Nokia-5800-xpressmusic.jpg," Wikipedia, February 1, 2009, http://en.wikipedia.org/wiki/File:Nokia-5800-xpressmusic.jpg. **8.4b:** William Hook, "Nokia N97 - Open," Flickr, photo taken August 11, 2009, www.flickr.com/photos/williamhook/3810779827/. **8.5:** Steve, "Java-scr-screenkeys.jpg," My Opera (blog), July 20, 2009, http://my.opera.com/SixtySixhundred/blog/?startidx=32. **8.6:** Apple, http://apple.com. **8.7:** John Blackburn, "iphone_titlebar_animation_1.jpg," Watching Apple (blog), November 19, 2009, http://watchingapple.com/2009/11/a-closer-look-at-iphone-transition-animations/. Annotated by the author. **8.8:** HTC, www.htc.com. **8.9:** Nokia, www.nokia.com. **8.10, 8.11:** Horace Dediu, "Google vs. Samsung," Asymco, November 14, 2012, www.asymco.com/2012/11/14/google-vs-samsung/. Used by permission. **8.12a,b:** Apple, http://apple.com. **8.13a–c:** Michael Friedman, "9987F371-E6E3-450A-AD6B-E588497591D6.jpeg," Philip Bloom (blog), February 7, 2012, http://philipbloom.net/2012/02/07/fcpxeditors/.

Index

prototypes
  creating, 192
  of Mint.com, 79
Psion, 146

Q

R

S

usability
in behavioral product design, 96
OpenID and, 55
usability data, 179
user-centered design, 184
User Experience Professionals
Association, 70
user interface
for Final Cut Pro X, 157
for Mint.com, 79–80
usernames, 57

V

validation, 3
variant manufacturing, by Nokia, 145
vehicle telematics, 22
vehicles
crash statistics, 53
dashboard origins, 20
electronic control units in, 22
test-driving, 48
touchscreen in, 52
U.S. government warnings about technology and safety, 52–53
venture capital, for Pownce, 116
video editing. *See* Final Cut Pro X
Vidoop, 62
Vimeo website, "Log in with Facebook" button, 64
visceral reactions to product, 96
visual design, high-quality, for Mint.com, 80
Volkswagen, VW Phaeton, 52

W

Wald, Abraham, 5–6
Walkman, 15
Walkman effect, 88
Wall Street Journal, 75, 90, 93
Wangen, Tim, 177
Wave. *See* Google Wave
Webloyalty, 128

websites, account sign-in process, 55
Wesabe, 16, 74–83
competition, 79–80
customer experience, 84
design, 75
hypothesis and testing, 195
key usability failure, 76–77
lessons, 83–85
Merchant Comparison screen, 74
opportunities and costs, 77
summary, 86
three-year battle, 81–83
Web 2.0 compliance, 78
whistle-blowing, 139
Wi-Fi, on Zune, 92
Wii (Nintendo), 100
wikis, 38
Wilson, Fred, 200
Winding Road website, 36, 194
Windows Phone, 95
Wired, 126
Wong, Yishan, 63
WordPerfect, 165
World War II, B-29 bombers, 5
worldwide communication, Twitter and, 114
Wrede, Oliver, 43

Y

Yadis, 57–58
Yahoo!, 172
OpenID and, 55
Yodlee, 77
Mint.com use of, 80

Z

ZDNet, 133
Zenlea, David, 36
Ziegler, Chris, 148
ZocDoc, 4
Zune. *See* Microsoft Zune media player

ACKNOWLEDGMENTS

This book was written over the course of two years and would not have been possible without the family, friends, and colleagues who supported my work. Though the topic of failure can be educational, interesting, and even thrilling at times, it can also be depressing, particularly when the failure is our own. I am deeply grateful to those who opened up and told me their stories, provided references, and took the time to review my work.

Thank you, Ulrike, for your love in spite of my failures. Thank you, Dad—and all of my family—for your support.

Thank you, Lou Rosenfeld, for working every day to be the best publisher in the world. Thanks to JoAnn Simony for the tough love editing I needed. Your thoughtfulness extended beyond merely editing to empathy with an author's long struggle. Thank you Karen Corbett, Ben Tedoff, and everyone at Rosenfeld Media for supporting quality publishing.

Thank you, Don Norman, for your gracious contribution, and thanks to Keith Instone, Michael Angeles, Scott Berkun, Paolo Borella, and Thomas Mann for technical reviews that made a material difference to my work. And special thanks to Lori Widelitz-Cavallucci for invaluable feedback and encouragement.

Thank you, Monica Camhi and friends, and Donna Fabyonic, for the generous gift of solitude.

Thanks to John McCrea, Chris Messina, Marc Hedlund, Preston Smalley, Phil Suessenguth, Daniel Burka, and David Evans for your courage to share difficult experiences.

Many people provided valuable feedback, ideas, interviews, and assistance. Thanks to John Ferrara, Mike Lee, Peter Jones, Tanya Rabourn, James Kalbach, Peter Van Dijck, Stephen P. Anderson, Lorelei Brown, Perry Hewitt, Jimmy Chandler, Austin Govella, Dave Moon, Nicolas Nova, Joe Bilman, Manuel Toscano, Karen McGrane, Peter Kaufman, Dan D'Ordine, Lindsay Lifrieri, Jared Spool, Sonja Cole, Fred Wilson, Rory Cumming, Brad Smith, Jennifer Jones, Andrew Hinton, Russ Unger, Camilla Grane, Gloria Bell, Belinda Lanks, Jason Grigsby, Andrew

Holz, Walter Mattingly, Michael Dila, John Blackburn, Bryce Johnson, Kevin Cheng, Patrick Lowery, Matthew Marco, Amy Lew, Mark Skinner, Michael McWatters, Kim Bieler, Whitney Quesenbery, Edward Loh, Bret Lider, Brant Cooper, Will Evans, Trevor Van Gorp, Peter Merholz, and the staff at the Montclair Public Library. I'm sure my faulty memory has misplaced some names, but those I missed also have my gratitude.

—Victor Lombardi, Montclair, New Jersey, May 2013

ABOUT THE AUTHOR

Victor Lombardi is an award-winning product designer who has contributed to more than 40 Internet projects since 1994. His writing has appeared in several publications, including *Fast Company* and *Interactions*, on topics ranging from generating concepts for new products to website evolution over time. Since 1999 he has published his ideas on business, design, and the Internet on his website, noisebetweenstations.com.

Victor earned a master's degree in music technology from New York University and a bachelor's degree in journalism from Rutgers University. He co-founded the Information Architecture Institute and the Overlap conference, and has taught design at the Parsons School of Design and the Pratt Institute. He lives in Montclair, New Jersey, with his wife, Ulrike, and their two children, Anna and Thomas.

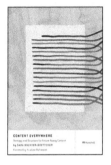

Content Everywhere: Strategy and Structure for Future-Ready Content

by Sara Wachter-Boettcher

December 2012

1-933820-87-X

www.rosenfeldmedia.com/books/content-everywhere/

Care about content? Better copy isn't enough. As devices and channels multiply—and as users expect to easily relate, share, and shift information—we need content that can go more places, more easily. This book will help you stop creating fixed, single-purpose content and start making it more future-ready, flexible, and reusable.

Design for Care: Innovating Healthcare Experience

by Peter Jones

June 2013

1-933820-23-3

www.rosenfeldmedia.com/books/design-for-care/

The world of healthcare is constantly evolving, ever increasing in complexity, costs, and stakeholders, and presenting huge challenges to policy making, decision making, and system design. In *Design for Care*, we'll show how service and information designers can work with practice professionals and patients/advocates to make a positive difference in healthcare.

Interviewing Users: How to Uncover Compelling Insights

by Steve Portigal

May 2013

1-933820-11-X

www.rosenfeldmedia.com/books/interviewing-users/

Interviewing is a foundational user research tool that people assume they already possess. Everyone can ask questions, right? Unfortunately, that's not the case. *Interviewing Users* provides invaluable interviewing techniques and tools that enable you to conduct informative interviews with anyone. You'll move from simply gathering data to uncovering powerful insights about people.

Make It So: Interaction Design Lessons from Science Fiction

by Nathan Shedroff and Christopher Noessel

September 2012

1-933820-98-5

www.rosenfeldmedia.com/books/make-it-so/

Many designers enjoy the interfaces seen in science fiction films and television shows. Freed from the rigorous constraints of designing for real users, sci-fi production designers develop blue-sky interfaces that are inspiring, humorous, and even instructive. By carefully studying these "outsider" user interfaces, designers can derive lessons that make their real-world designs more cutting edge and successful.

The Mobile Frontier: A Guide for Designing Mobile Experiences
by Rachel Hinman
June 2012
1-933820-55-1

Mobile user experience is a new frontier. Untethered from a keyboard and mouse, this rich design space is ripe with opportunities to invent new and more human ways for people to interact with information. *The Mobile Frontier* will help you navigate this unfamiliar and fast-changing landscape, and inspire you to explore the possibilities that mobile technology presents.

Playful Design: Creating Game Experiences in Everyday Interfaces
by John Ferrara
May 2012
1-933820-14-4

Game design is a sibling discipline to software and Web design, but they're siblings that grew up in different houses. They have much more in common than their perceived distinction typically suggests, and user experience practitioners can realize enormous benefit by exploiting the solutions that games have found to the real problems of design. This book will show you how.

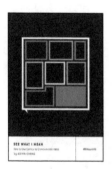

See What I Mean: How to Use Comics to Communicate Ideas
by Kevin Cheng
December 2012
1-933820-27-6

Comics can provide your organization with an exciting and effective alternative to slogging through requirements documents and long reports. In *See What I Mean*, Kevin will walk you step by step through the process of using comics to communicate, and provide examples from industry leaders who have already adopted this method.

Storytelling for User Experience: Crafting Stories for Better Design
by Whitney Quesenbery and Kevin Brooks
April 2010
1-933820-47-0

We all use stories to communicate, explore, persuade, and inspire. In user experience, stories help us to understand our users, learn about their goals, explain our research, and demonstrate our design ideas. In this book, Quesenbery and Brooks teach you how to craft and tell your own unique stories to improve your designs.